PSYCHOLOGICAL ASSESSMENT
AND
REPORT WRITING

PSYCHOLOGICAL ASSESSMENT
AND
REPORT WRITING

KAREN GOLDFINGER
Licensed Clinical Psychologist, Connecticut

ANDREW M. POMERANTZ
Southern Illinois University Edwardsville

Los Angeles • London • New Delhi • Singapore • Washington DC

Disclaimer

"All case descriptions in this volume are disguised composites or fabrications."

For information:

SAGE Publications, Inc.
2455 Teller Road
Thousand Oaks, California 91320
E-mail: order@sagepub.com

SAGE Publications India Pvt. Ltd.
B 1/I 1 Mohan Cooperative
    Industrial Area
Mathura Road, New Delhi 110 044
India

SAGE Publications Ltd.
1 Oliver's Yard
55 City Road
London EC1Y 1SP
United Kingdom

SAGE Publications Asia-Pacific Pte. Ltd.
33 Pekin Street #02-01
Far East Square
Singapore 048763

Printed in the United States of America

Library of Congress Cataloging-in-Publication Data

Goldfinger, Karen.
Psychological assessment and report writing/Karen Goldfinger, Andrew M. Pomerantz.
     p. cm.
Includes bibliographical references and index.
ISBN 978-1-4129-6096-0 (pbk.)
   1. Psychology—Methodology. 2. Behavioral assessment. 3. Report writing.
I. Pomerantz, Andrew M. II. Title.

BF38.5.G65 2009
150.28'7—dc22   2008038168

This book is printed on acid-free paper.

09   10   11   12   13   10   9   8   7   6   5   4   3   2   1

Acquisitions Editor:	Erik Evans
Editorial Assistant:	Sarita Sarak
Production Editor:	Astrid Virding
Copy Editor:	QuADS Prepress (P) Ltd.
Typesetter:	C&M Digitals (P) Ltd.
Proofreader:	Anne Rogers
Indexer:	Will Ragsdale
Cover Designer:	Gail Buschman
Marketing Manager:	Stephanie Adams

Contents

Acknowledgments

Acknowledgments From Karen Goldfinger

This book could not have been completed without the help of numerous colleagues and friends. Stacey Sparks, a writer and editor, was my first collaborator and helped me shape my ideas into book form. Lynda Smith, Lynn Abrahamson, and Joy Alter Hubel were enthusiastic supporters from the beginning. Jeff Turner reviewed the work in its early stages and gave me needed advice about going forward with a proposal. My husband, Marinus Tijl, helped me think through the most complicated material, and the resulting chapters would not have been nearly as effective without his input. My first editor at Sage, Cheri Dellelo, was instrumental in putting the pieces together to make this book happen, and Erik Evans saw it through to the finished text. I thank them both for their effort and advice. I have learned much of what I know about assessment from my clients and the people who referred them to me, and I am grateful for the privilege of having worked with so many people over the years. I learned about the needs of students from my supervisees and the doctoral students who took assessment with me at the University of Hartford, and I thank them for teaching me. Finally, this book would never have been completed without the hard work and talent of my coauthor, Andy Pomerantz, and I am so appreciative of his willingness to collaborate with me on this project.

Acknowledgments From Andy Pomerantz

First and foremost, I would like to thank Karen Goldfinger for the opportunity to participate on this book. I truly appreciate her vision, expertise, and collaborative spirit. My wife, Melissa, always inspires me and supports all my efforts through her love and friendship. My kids, Benjamin and Daniel, bring joy to my life and meaning to all my work. My parents, Bill and Carol Pomerantz, have provided a lifetime of love and support for all my efforts. Cheri Dellelo of Sage facilitated my involvement in this project, and Erik Evans of Sage provided great insight and support—many, many thanks to both. I have learned a great deal from Mary Ellen Lepionka about text-book authorship, and to her I am indebted. The SIUE Department of Psychology allows my writing to thrive. My graduate professors and supervisors from Saint Louis University and my undergraduate professors at Washington University sparked my interest in clinical psychology. The reviewers of the prospectus and chapter drafts of this book—listed below—provided valuable feedback and enhanced the book in numerous ways:

Alisha Ali, New York University

Soledad Arguelles-Borge, Nova Southeastern University

Meredith Coles, Binghamton University

Terry Diamanduros, Georgia Southern University

Giselle B. Esquivel, Fordham University

Thomas P. Harding, Binghamton University

Carolyn Keatinge, Pepperdine University

Richard E. Mattson, Auburn University

Paul C. McCabe, Brooklyn College, City University of New York

Adam W. Meade, North Carolina State University

Wendy Quinton, University at Buffalo, State University of New York

Serina Rosenkjar, California Lutheran University

Leonard Simms, University at Buffalo, State University of New York

Stephen R. Yerian, Wright State University

And finally, I thank my clients, especially my assessment clients, from whom I have learned a great deal.

CHAPTER 1

Introduction

A Brief History of Psychological Testing and Assessment and Some Definitions

Margaret came into the psychologist's office wearing an old-fashioned housedress, the kind that is a faded plaid and has snaps instead of buttons. She was accompanied by a man in a business suit, her son Peter, who told the psychologist, "My mother's doctor told me to bring her in for the appointment and that you would know what to do." He was right. Dr. Shaw had called earlier in the week and told the psychologist that he was concerned about Margaret's memory and wanted her tested to rule out dementia. On the day of the appointment, the psychologist had Margaret and Peter complete the necessary paperwork. She began the assessment with interviews. She then gave Margaret a brief battery of cognitive and memory tests and a self-report depression inventory. When they were finished, she made a follow-up appointment with Margaret and Peter to review the findings, and later in the week she prepared a written report to send to Dr. Shaw.

Psychologists routinely conduct assessments, such as this one with Margaret, to understand behavior, make decisions about people, manage risk, and develop treatment plans. Human beings have made efforts toward these goals for centuries, across civilizations and cultures. One can imagine that, even in aboriginal tribes, leaders select individuals to fulfill roles based on a relevant set of criteria, whether it is how fast they can run, how accurately they can hit a target, or their leadership abilities. We know that tests of one sort or another were used in both ancient Greece and ancient China to select individuals to fulfill roles important to those cultures (see Matarazzo, 1990).

Psychology is a relatively new profession, but from its earliest days, assessment of people to make decisions about them was one of its functions. Standardized tests of intellectual functioning were developed early in the 20th century to make decisions about educational placements, and personality assessment was first used in the early 1900s for employment selection. During World War I, soldiers were famously administered intelligence testing in a group format, the Army Alpha and

Beta series. The Rorschach was introduced in 1921, the Wechsler scales in 1939, and the MMPI (Minnesota Multiphasic Personality Inventory) in 1940. These instruments, in revised forms, are the most widely used tests in psychology today (Camara, Nathan, & Puente, 2000). Behavior rating scales, self-report inventories (e.g., Beck Depression Inventory II, or BDI-II), and structured interviews are relatively new additions to the field and growing in popularity among clinicians (Kamphaus, Petoskey, & Rowe, 2000). A selected list of psychological tests used with children, compiled by these authors, includes 83 items. Camara et al. (2000) selected 120 tests to be used in a survey of clinicians (clinical and neuropsychologists) and added 9 more that were written in by clinicians. New tests are developed every year and old ones are revised. A quick look at publishers' test catalogs suggests that psychological testing is a growth industry.

Psychological *testing*—the act of administering, scoring, and interpreting results of a test that measures any one of a number of psychological functions, such as cognitive ability, memory, or personality traits—is a straightforward process. Psychological *assessment* is not. In psychological testing, the interpretation of results is limited to description of the meaning of a score, and the only other data that are relevant are concerned with the validity and reliability of that score based on the relevance of normative data and the test subject's behavior. However, scores on an individual test, no matter how carefully it is chosen, administered, scored, and interpreted, rarely provide sufficient information on which to base significant decisions or an understanding of complex problems. In the reasonably straightforward scenario described above, Margaret would be poorly served if the psychologist gave her a memory test, or even a battery of memory tests, and interpreted the results without benefit of interviewing her and her son. Perhaps she has depression, low intellectual functioning, or an anxiety disorder, any of which might affect test results. Furthermore, careful interviews of Margaret and Peter add depth and ecological validity to the findings and allow the psychologist to provide useful and meaningful recommendations to Dr. Shaw and the patient's family. As Meyer et al. (2001) note, "A psychological test is a dumb tool, and the worth of the tool cannot be separated from the sophistication of the clinician who draws inferences from it and then communicates with patients and other professionals" (p. 153).

Psychological assessment, in contrast to psychological testing,

> is concerned with the clinician who takes a variety of test scores, generally obtained from multiple test methods, and considers the data in the context of history, referral information, and observed behavior to understand the person being evaluated, to answer the referral questions, and then to communicate findings to the patient, his or her significant others, and referral sources. (Meyer et al., 2001, p. 143)

Matarazzo (1990), then president of the American Psychological Association, noted in his presidential address that "assessment of intelligence, personality, or type or level of impairment is a highly complex operation that involves extracting diagnostic meaning from an individual's personal history and objectively recorded test scores" (p. 1000).

Difficulties in Mastering Psychological Assessment

Learning how to administer, score, and interpret test results is a challenge in itself, and a psychologist needs to know a great deal more to conduct a psychological assessment. It is not a simple task, and for many students, one that they never embrace. Students need to know the following:

- Test and measurement theory
- The specifics of administering, scoring, and interpreting a variety of tests
- Theories of personality, development, and abnormal behavior
- Details related to the purpose and context of the evaluation, such as legal issues in a forensic evaluation or special education regulations in an assessment for a school
- How to conduct an interview and mental status examination
- What to look for when they observe the client's behavior
- The legal and ethical regulations governing their work

They also need to have a working knowledge of psychopathology, including *DSM-IV* diagnosis and, at least at a rudimentary level, brain functioning, and they need to bring effective thinking and communication skills to the task.

The psychologist faced with evaluating Margaret, the client described above, additionally needs to know the following:

- What to ask the referring party, Dr. Shaw, and what to tell Dr. Shaw about the evaluation process
- What to tell Margaret and Peter about the assessment
- How to develop rapport with Margaret and Peter
- What to ask in the interview and how to ask it
- How to choose which tests to administer and strategies for administering the tests to someone who may have significant deficits
- How to interpret test results and integrate test results with other information in order to address referral questions
- How to develop suitable recommendations
- How to write a formal report and provide feedback to Margaret and her son

It is not surprising that students often respond to the challenges of learning assessment skills defensively by avoiding it ("Why do I have to learn this? . . . I'm never going to do assessments . . . they are a waste of time.") or by overstating their abilities ("Assessment is easy; why do we have to spend so much time learning and practicing it?"). There is a lot to learn. The benefits of learning to conduct effective assessments go beyond writing a good report for an assigned client and obtaining a strong recommendation from a supervisor. First, developing a thorough understanding of complex human behavior and being able to write about it effectively is a highly useful skill in all psychological work, even that which does not involve formal assessment. Second, the practice in thinking and communication skills that assessment requires enhances the student's professionalism. Third, students who are capable and comfortable in conducting assessments have expanded career opportunities. Finally, better preparation in assessment will allow *all* psychologists to skillfully conduct assessments. Only then will psychological assessments be of consistently high quality.

Purpose and Goals of This Book

Beginning psychologists typically learn assessment skills through didactic instruction and supervised experience. They take courses in test and measurement theory, personality, psychopathology, and assessment, and they may complete one or more assessments under supervision in coursework or practicum settings.

This text provides the structure, guidance, and instruction students require to take what they learn in the classroom and apply it in a clinical, forensic, or educational setting. That is, this text serves as a bridge between the theoretical and practical instruction of the classroom and its application in real-world settings. For example, a student may be skillful in administering and interpreting tests and have a good grasp of psychopathology, but faced with Margaret and her son, or any other assessment client, the student needs to understand the context of the evaluation, know what information is needed and how to gather it, know how to integrate all the obtained information to draw conclusions and make recommendations, and know how to write a persuasive, accurate, readable, and useful report. This text equips students to do all these tasks with skill, professionalism, and confidence.

The text accomplishes its goals by using a step-by-step model of assessment, providing instruction, guidelines, and examples at each point. A schematic of the model is shown in Figure 1.1.

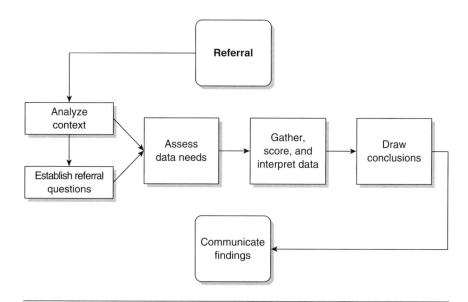

Figure 1.1   A Model for Psychological Assessment

In the case of Margaret, the model works as follows:

1. *Referral:* Margaret was referred by her internist, Dr. Shaw. He sees a lot of elderly patients and has made several other referrals to the same psychologist. He wants to know the following: Are the results of tests of memory and cognitive functioning consistent with dementia? Do they show a decline from premorbid functioning? If so, what is the impact of any decline on Margaret's day-to-day life, and what are the chances that the apparent decline is due to other factors, especially depression? All Dr. Shaw said, however, is "I would like you to test Margaret to rule out dementia."

2. *The context of the referral:* Dr. Shaw made the referral because Peter, Margaret's son, expressed concern about his mother's memory problems. Peter will pay for the evaluation privately, but the report will go to Dr. Shaw. Peter is concerned about his mother's day-to-day functioning and ability to live independently. Dr. Shaw wants to confirm a diagnosis of dementia before trying a new medication.

3. *Information needed to address the referral questions:* To answer the implicit and explicit referral questions, the psychologist needs (a) an estimate of Margaret's premorbid cognitive and memory functioning; (b) her history of emotional problems and signs and symptoms of depression or anxiety; (c) results of tests of memory and cognitive functioning; and (d) knowledge about Margaret's everyday behaviors, the demands of her present lifestyle, and her ability to meet the demands. She also needs to be knowledgeable about the effects of normal aging on cognition, memory, emotional functioning, and everyday life.

4. *Gathering the data:* The psychologist conducts a semistructured interview to obtain the premorbid history, assess for signs and symptoms of depression and anxiety, and find out about Margaret's daily life. She reviews Margaret's medical record and interviews Margaret and Peter separately and together. She administers the BDI-II and subtests of the Wechsler Memory Scale-Third Edition (WMS-III) and Wechsler Adult Intelligence Scale-Third Edition (WAIS-III) to Margaret. She makes sure that the tests have norms that are appropriate to Margaret's age. She uses reference materials to ensure that she is interpreting the data correctly and not confusing dementia with normal aging. She also takes into account any cultural issues that may be relevant, such as race or ethnicity.

5. *Using the data to answer referral questions:* The psychologist evaluates what she learned from the background information and history and what she observed about Margaret's behavior during the interviews and while she was taking the tests. She decides if the test results are valid and what they tell her about Margaret's cognitive and memory functions. She determines if the results from all assessment domains are consistent and if she knows everything she needs to in order to answer the referral questions. Then she decides if the results are consistent with dementia and, if so, how it affects Margaret's daily life. If not, are there some other problems that need to be addressed? In either case, she develops recommendations that would be helpful to Margaret and her family.

6. *Communicating the findings:* The psychologist communicates her findings to Margaret and her son in a follow-up appointment and prepares a report for Dr. Shaw.

This text reviews each of these sections at length, alerting readers to myriad issues that he might not have considered and providing "how-to" instructions each step of the way.

There are important aspects of conducting an assessment that the text does not address. We don't discuss how to prepare a client for assessment or how to provide verbal feedback to a client after the assessment. Both of these tasks are extremely important, and we recommend that they be reviewed closely in supervision, focusing on specific cases the student is taking on. We also don't discuss conducting assessments of clients prior to initiating therapy with them or in the course of therapy. These are assessment practices that are beyond the scope of this book.

Also beyond the scope of this book is an extensive exploration of evidence-based assessment practices. Of course, as scientists we recognize the importance of empirical evidence in all aspects of the practice of psychology, including assessment. Furthermore, we recognize that, especially in very recent years, many sources of information on evidence-based assessment have emerged. For example, guidance is available for evidence-based assessment of learning disabilities (e.g., Fletcher, Francis, Morris, & Lyon, 2005), anxiety disorders (e.g., Antony & Rowa, 2005), depression (e.g., Klein, Dougherty, & Olino, 2005), attention-deficit/hyperactivity disorder (e.g., Pelham, Fabiano, & Massetti, 2005), and other presenting problems (e.g., Barlow, 2005; Hunsley & Mash, 2007). We encourage readers to become familiar with these and other sources of information on evidence-based assessment and to stay current regarding research on psychological assessment. It is also important to remember, however, that clinical expertise customized to individual characteristics of individual clients—as emphasized in this book—should complement such research. As stated by the APA Presidential Task Force on Evidence-Based Practice (2006), "evidence based practice in psychology is the integration of the best available research *with clinical expertise in the context of patient characteristics, culture, and preferences* [italics added]" (p. 284). Many of the topics addressed in this book, including some aspects of gathering information and virtually all aspects of report writing, have been subjected to little or no empirical study. For example, there is currently no body of empirical literature suggesting that certain report writing practices or decisions are more "evidence based" than others. So we emphasize clinical expertise in the context of situational and personal variables that may be entirely unique to a particular client.

How to Use This Book

The text is designed for use in a classroom setting or more informally in individual or group supervision. It can also be used independently by psychologists who wish to improve or refine their assessment skills. It prepares students for supervised work and supplements supervision; it is not a substitute for supervision. Supervisors can assign chapters or sections when they detect a weakness in the student's preparation or skill set, making them free to focus on other aspects of the student's work.

For the beginning assessment student, chapters in the text are intended to be read sequentially, because each skill set builds on the one introduced previously. If students do not understand the importance of evaluating the context of a referral and how to go about making that evaluation, they will not be prepared to determine which information is needed to answer referral questions. Similarly, if they don't identify and gather all the necessary data, making sure they are valid and accurate, they can't use the data to accurately answer the referral questions.

If the information in previous chapters has already been mastered, each chapter can be reviewed as a separate entity. Some students may need to review particular chapters several times to master the material, while others may grasp concepts more readily, so students may benefit from working at their own pace with the goal of mastery of the concepts in each chapter by the time they are through with the text. At that point, students will be well prepared to take on assessment clients under supervision and to make good use of supervision to refine their work, especially the complicated tasks of case formulation and preparation of a written report.

Chapters and Their Contents

The text is divided into four sections. Part I contains two chapters. As we have seen, Chapter 1 offers a brief history of psychological testing, defines psychological assessment, describes the difficulties students encounter in learning the skills of assessment, and presents a model for instruction of assessment skills. Chapter 2, "Context: The Framework for the Report," describes a systematic approach that students can use to thoroughly evaluate the context in which a referral takes place. The contextual factors considered include implicit and explicit referral questions, the audience for the findings, who initiated and who is paying for the assessment, the anticipated functions of the report, client and clinician attributes, and systems issues. Students are strongly encouraged to review each of these factors in the early stages of every assessment case.

Part II is concerned with gathering information and drawing conclusions from it. Chapter 3, "Gathering Information," discusses the functions of information and the challenges in gathering it. The chapter goes on to describe six steps for gathering information and presents a case example. Chapter 4, "Gathering Information: Measures of Intellectual, Academic, and Neuropsychological Functioning," reviews commonly used measures of cognitive ability, academic achievement, and neuropsychological functioning, including the Wechsler, Stanford-Binet, and Woodcock-Johnson batteries; alternative measures such as the Peabody Picture Vocabulary Test; short forms of intelligence tests; and some specific tests of memory, attention, visual-spatial skills, and other neuropsychological functions. The focus of the chapter is on providing clinically relevant guidelines, applicable to real-world settings, for choosing and administering tests and interpreting the results. Chapter 5, "Gathering Information: Measures of Personality," reviews widely used objective and projective measures of personality functioning, focusing on the most recent editions of the Minnesota Multiphasic Personality Inventory (MMPI), Millon Clinical Multiaxial Inventory (MCMI), Personality Assessment Inventory

(PAI), NEO Personality Inventory-Revised (NEO-PI-R), Rorschach Inkblot Method, and Thematic Apperception Test (TAT). Each instrument, or group of instruments, is discussed at length with special attention paid to empirical findings and controversies, advantages and disadvantages of the instrument, and applications in real-world settings. Chapter 6, "Gathering Information: Clinical Interviews, Review of Records, and Measures of Behavioral and Emotional Functioning," considers a range of techniques for assessing social, emotional, and behavioral functioning, including interviews, rating scales, and behavioral assessment strategies. Methods are reviewed at length with the goal of providing guidelines for thinking about, choosing, and using the techniques wisely in real-world assessment situations. Chapter 7, "Drawing Conclusions," addresses the complicated question of how to integrate data to answer referral questions. This chapter takes the readers through several steps designed to help them sort through the information that was gathered. It provides instructions on organizing the data, dealing with disparities and incidental findings, summarizing the findings, and developing recommendations. Several case examples make the process clear.

Part III of the book focuses on report writing. Chapter 8, "Form and Content of the Report," begins with a discussion of the value of a written report. It identifies alternative methods for structuring the report and reviews the contents of each section, using a case example. Chapter 9, "Writing Style," reviews a number of concepts related to writing style in psychological reports, including clarity, accuracy, persuasiveness, and finding one's voice. Among other topics, it discusses the importance of writing for an audience, distinguishing between opinions and facts, problems of tense, and eliminating jargon. The chapter also reviews research on persuasive communication and how it applies to the psychological assessment report.

Part IV has a single chapter, Chapter 10, "Ethics of Assessment and Report Writing," and it reviews common ethical problems faced by clinicians in the field and guidelines for their resolution. These are amply illustrated through case examples.

Conclusion

Psychological assessment is the art and science of using psychological tests and other sources of data to answer questions about human behavior. This book provides students with the background they need to conduct effective psychological assessments in "real-world" clinical, educational, or forensic settings. It offers a step-by-step model of assessment, from meeting the client and thinking through the context of the assessment to gathering and integrating data and writing a report. Students are provided direction, guidance, and case examples to help them master each component of the model. They are encouraged to apply what they learn to their own cases and to use critical thinking skills throughout the assessment process. By the time they complete the textbook, students will be well prepared to conduct psychological assessments under supervision with skill and confidence. Furthermore, as they move forward in their careers as professional psychologists, students will continue to benefit from having developed these skills, regardless of their field of specialization.

2

Context

The Framework for the Report

An assessment is not completed in a vacuum. The context of a case makes it unique, and the psychologist's understanding of the context gives the assessment relevance. Think about the first psychological "assessments" graduate students conduct. The purpose of the assessment is for the student to learn from the experience, and often the assessment is performed on neighbors or friends. Clearly, for the neighbor or friend, this is a markedly different context for assessment than one in which he is assessed at school for a learning disability or at the psychologist's office for attention-deficit/hyperactivity disorder (ADHD). The person undergoing the assessment is the same, but the context for the assessment makes it a very different experience for both the psychologist and the "client." The context affects the choice of assessment procedures, the relationship between the psychologist and the client, the interpretation of results, the conclusions that are drawn from the assessment, and the final report.

Consider the difference between a parent involved in a divorce undergoing projective testing by her therapist in the initial stages of psychotherapy and the same client undergoing projective testing in the course of a child custody evaluation by a forensic evaluator. Anxiety and defensiveness are normal responses to the latter context, while openness and lack of inhibition might be appropriate responses to the former. Conclusions drawn from test results must take these factors into account. In the end, psychological reports about a single client vary, often markedly, depending on the context of the evaluation. They should. Conclusions might also vary depending on which psychologist conducts the assessment. However, these variations should be slight and related to form, not substance.

The following are useful factors to consider when thinking about the context of an assessment. It is essential that they be reviewed in every assessment case.

Initiation and Funding of the Assessment

Clients are referred for assessment through numerous pathways. A client might be referred by a primary-care physician due to unresolved psychosomatic complaints or by a medical specialist in preparation for surgery. A client could be referred by a therapist due to unremitting depression or by an entire treatment team that wants a differential diagnosis. Children and adolescents are often referred by special education directors, school administrators, teachers, or parents due to academic or behavioral problems at school. However, they might also be referred by probation officers, attorneys, or judges of the juvenile court, or by pediatricians concerned about their mental health or learning problems. Attorneys might refer parents and children in custody disputes, defendants in criminal trials, or plaintiffs filing personal injury lawsuits.

The telephone call, letter, e-mail, fax, or conversation initiating the referral is only the starting point for determining who wants to know something about the client and why she wants to know it. It is up to the psychologist conducting the assessment to sort out the details. For example, a child might be referred to a psychologist in private practice by the special education director of a local school district because of a temporary understaffing of psychologists or, alternatively, because of concerns about risk and liability. A referral might be made so as to minimize conflict with litigious parents in an already heated situation, or the child in question might present complex problems that are beyond the expertise of staff members. The referral may be initiated in each case by a simple phone call, but the psychologist needs to determine the reasons for the referral, perhaps through another phone conversation or by studying the child's records. Sorting out the reasons for referral will be discussed in more detail below.

The source of funding for the assessment is also an important factor to consider. An assessment may be paid for privately by a client or his or her family members, by the client's insurance company, or by taxpayers through the school budget or the courts. The funding often determines "ownership" of the assessment and its primary audience. For example, an assessment paid for by a school district often serves a different purpose than one paid for by a parent. Jane is a 10th grader at a local public high school. Her parents are concerned about her academic performance. They have chosen not to request an evaluation through the school for several reasons, including Jane's embarrassment, and the chance that other students would find out she is struggling, the length of time the evaluation would take to complete, and a mild suspicion about what the school would do with the information that was gathered. Jane's parents want to be in control of the process and are willing to pay for it. Their goal is for Jane to be happy and successful. The report will belong to them, and they will use it to understand Jane's needs and to advocate for Jane with the school system. John is a 10th grader at the same high school. His parents requested that the school conduct an assessment due to his poor academic performance, and school personnel agreed. Schools are required to conduct an assessment at the request of parents in many circumstances. The school's goal is to meet its legal obligations, satisfy the request of John's parents, and provide John with an appropriate educational program. School personnel may hope that John will be happy and successful, but that is not their primary goal in conducting the assessment. Note that regardless of the source of payment for an assessment, it is wise for the psychologist to clarify with all involved parties the access (or lack thereof) that each will have to the assessment results.

Once it is determined who initiated and who is paying for the assessment, it usually becomes apparent whether the client is a willing participant. An assessment may be viewed by the client, even before beginning, as a positive experience designed to help or as a frightening requirement that he would much prefer to avoid. A client referred for assessment by his therapist might be anxious about the assessment process, but he understands that the process is meant to provide a solution to a problem. In contrast, for a client ordered by a judge to undergo an assessment preliminary to a competency hearing or as part of a child custody evaluation, the assessment is likely to be experienced as coercive and anxiety provoking.

Identifying those responsible for initiating and funding an assessment, and developing an idea about the extent to which the client's participation is voluntary, should be done early in the assessment process. The psychologist needs to be able to answer the following questions:

- Who referred the client for assessment?
- Who is paying for it?
- Is the client a willing participant in the assessment process?

These are usually not difficult questions to answer, and they are a good place to start defining the contextual factors relevant to a case.

Why Was the Client Referred? Implicit and Explicit Reasons for Referral

Occasionally, the reason for a referral for psychological assessment is straightforward. A student might be referred for an assessment of intellectual functioning, a psychiatric patient for clarification of diagnosis, or a psychotherapy patient for treatment recommendations. However, more often than not, the reason for referral is complex, multilayered, or simply different from what the psychologist initially expected. A full understanding of the reason for referral guides the psychologist in all phases of the assessment, including the interview, the review of records, the choice of assessment instruments, observation of the subject of the assessment, and preparation of the written report.

Often a referral is made for administrative rather than clinical reasons. The purpose of the assessment, for example, might be to determine if the client is eligible for certain services or accommodations, or whether he will be admitted to specific clinical or educational programs. In such instances, the assessment serves a gatekeeping function. In other situations, the assessment has a clinical function—to improve a treatment plan, clarify a diagnosis, or learn more about a client's personality. Assessments may also serve educational needs—for example, by clarifying a student's cognitive strengths and weaknesses or academic achievement levels in different subjects so that an appropriate educational plan may be developed. An assessment can have a forensic purpose, serving the needs of the legal system. Assessments serve other functions, too, for example, in personnel selection or leadership development. The psychologist should always make an effort to determine if the assessment is meant to serve clinical, educational, gatekeeping, forensic, or a combination of these or other functions. For example, the assessment might indicate that a client is eligible for academic accommodations (gatekeeping function), recommend specific remediation strategies (educational function), and recommend treatment for anxiety (clinical function).

It is important to note that the reason for referral can easily be misunderstood by the psychologist. Here are two examples. (1) Shelly is a 22-year-old patient in a psychiatric hospital. Her psychiatrist referred her for assessment to clarify her diagnosis. The psychologist assigned to conduct the assessment did not understand why Shelly had been referred, because everybody who worked with her in the hospital, including the psychiatrist, felt certain that she had bipolar disorder. The psychologist looked into the case further and found that the outside agencies responsible for providing treatment for Shelly had declined the hospital's request for intensive services. Shelly had a lot of drug problems, and the outside agency attributed her difficulties to substance abuse. The psychiatrist wanted the assessment done to add "ammunition" to the treatment team's efforts to obtain appropriate community services for Shelly, so that she could be safely discharged from the hospital setting. Thus, the assessment served a gatekeeping function. (2) Pam is a 14-year-old student who was referred for assessment by her parents. She did not do well academically in her first year in a private high school, and the school suggested that she have an educational assessment. That seemed straightforward to the psychologist, who initially thought that the goal of the assessment was to understand Pam's academic difficulties so that they could be addressed. However, on careful questioning of Pam's parents, the psychologist determined that the school required the assessment before it would allow her to return the next year. School officials wanted to waive the foreign language requirement for Pam and make some other accommodations, and that could not be done without documentation of a learning problem.

Another possibility is that the assessment has a surprising, hidden, or tacit, agenda. For example, when Anthony was referred by his attorney for an assessment of depression, the psychologist initially assumed, incorrectly, that the attorney thought Anthony was depressed and in need of treatment. On further questioning of the attorney about the referral, the psychologist found out that Anthony had been ordered by the judge to participate in psychotherapy due to a history of depression. His attorney disagreed with that disposition and did not believe that he was in need of treatment. If there were no findings of depression, the attorney could work to reverse the court order.

Explicit referral questions are those that are clearly stated by the referral source. Implicit referral questions are those that are ferreted out by the psychologist, as she considers all aspects of a case. Thus, the explicit referral question in Anthony's case is, "Does Anthony have depression?" The implicit question is, "Does Anthony need court-ordered treatment for depression?" In Shelly's case, the explicit question is,

"Does Shelly have bipolar disorder?" The implicit questions are, "How certain is the diagnosis of bipolar disorder?" "Could her symptoms be due to drug abuse?" "Does she meet eligibility requirements for an outpatient treatment program for young adults who have bipolar disorder?" For Pam, the explicit question is, "What will help her be more successful in school?" while the implicit question is, "Does she qualify for a foreign language waiver and other academic accommodations?" The implicit referral questions are extremely important to address, because the report will not meet the needs of the client or the referring party otherwise.

The psychologist determines the explicit and implicit referral questions through a sort of detective work, via interviews with the client, the referring party, or other individuals who have background information, and through a review of any records. She might also consult with colleagues who have experience in similar assessment contexts. The psychologist might also have a brief dialogue with the referrer that would go something like this:

Psychologist: I understand that you referred Anthony for evaluation of depression. Tell me more about how that will be helpful.

Attorney: Well, he doesn't seem depressed to me, and he keeps complaining about having to see his therapist.

Psychologist: So you don't really think that he has depression?

Attorney: No, and I don't think he needs to be in treatment.

Psychologist: Why doesn't he talk about it with his therapist? A lot of people just decide not to continue.

Attorney: The therapy was ordered by the judge the last time he was in court. His mother insisted that Anthony was depressed and needed to be in therapy, but really they just don't get along. I have not been in contact with his therapist, so I don't know how he sees it.

Psychologist: Do you have any other concerns about Anthony?

Attorney: Not really. He does very well in most areas. I don't think he needs to be in treatment unless he wants to go, and he doesn't.

Psychologist: Okay, I understand . . . (the psychologist goes ahead and makes the appointment).

If the psychologist had not been interested in the context of the assessment, the dialogue might have gone like this:

Psychologist: I understand that you referred Anthony for evaluation of depression. When do you need the report?

Attorney: His next court date is in 2 months, so if I get a report in 6 weeks, it should be OK.

Psychologist: That's not a problem (the psychologist goes ahead and makes the appointment.)

Obviously, a report completed after the first conversation will better meet the needs of Anthony and his attorney, regardless of the findings.

Sometimes more extensive "detective work" is needed. In Shelly's case, the psychologist needed to talk with several members of the treatment team as well as a representative of the outside agency and read several pages of progress notes before figuring out the implicit referral question. She knew to look for one, because the explicit referral question did not make sense. No one on the hospital staff doubted that Shelly had bipolar disorder, and patients like Shelly were not typically referred for assessment when the diagnosis was clear-cut. The psychologist kept looking until she had figured out why she was being asked to do the assessment, until it made sense. (Furthermore, until she figured out how the assessment would help Shelly, she couldn't get her to cooperate with testing. After she knew how it could help, she presented the rationale more effectively, and Shelly completed all that she asked without a problem.)

How does the psychologist know when he fully conceptualizes both the explicit and the implicit referral questions? The referral must make sense in light of the client's history and current life problems. It is important to search for information with an open mind. Ask open-ended questions of referral sources, helping them explain what they need and want. Defensiveness on the part of the person making the referral is not helpful. Whoever made the referral is asking for help; the psychologist has to sort out what it is that person needs and the best way to provide it, and this must be done artfully.

These are the key factors to remember in regard to explicit and implicit referral questions:

• There are often implicit as well as explicit referral questions. If the explicit referral question, the one first indicated by the referral source, does not make sense, it is essential to keep looking for the implicit or hidden questions.

• For every case, it is vital to determine if the assessment is meant to serve clinical, educational, gatekeeping, or a combination of these (or other) functions.

• Bear in mind that it is easy to misunderstand the reason for a referral. The psychologist must keep an open mind and use due diligence to ensure that he fully understands the purpose of the assessment.

• The payoff for fully and accurately conceptualizing the referral question is a report that meets the needs of the client and the referral source.

Primary and Secondary Audiences for the Findings

At the end of the assessment, results will be shared with one or more parties in person, on the telephone, and/or in writing. Communicating the results of a psychological assessment is, in fact, an ethical obligation (American Psychological Association, 2002). A review of results can provide a powerful clinical intervention. As the psychologist explains procedures, the way he came to conclusions, and the conclusions themselves, the client and his family members may hear for the first time that he has a mental health or learning problem that explains his difficulties or that his problems do not warrant any such diagnosis. The client and his family may also learn what can be done about the problem, so that the assessment process becomes a first, hopeful step in a process of recovery or adaptation.

In most situations, the psychologist also prepares a written report. The primary audience for the findings is the person (or persons) to whom the original report will be sent; often this is the person who made the referral. The report should be prepared with this audience in mind. It must address the needs of this audience and be written in language, and have a conceptual structure, that this audience understands. However, the report is likely to have one or more other readers in its near or distant future. This is the secondary audience, and it should not be neglected.

Ellen, a 10-year-old girl in the fifth grade, was referred through a planning and placement team (PPT) meeting at her school for an assessment of cognitive functioning as part of an initial assessment to determine her eligibility for special education. A report of the findings was prepared by the school psychologist and sent to the members of the PPT, including Ellen's classroom teachers, the principal, a special education teacher, and her parents. Copies of the report were also placed in Ellen's special education records, and an educational evaluator and school psychologist will review the report when Ellen is in the eighth grade and scheduled for reassessment. Ellen's parents are thinking about providing a copy of the report to Ellen's therapist, and they might give one to her pediatrician, too. Ellen might also be able to access the report when she gets older. In this case, the primary audience—the audience the report is directed to—is the PPT, and the secondary audience includes the therapist, the pediatrician, and perhaps Ellen.

In this somewhat complicated but not unusual situation, the report should be directed toward school personnel but written in a manner that is understandable and acceptable to Ellen's parents. The psychologist should also be aware that there are probable secondary audiences for the report and should take these into account by clearly describing the purpose of the assessment and its procedures.

Juan is a 50-year-old man about to undergo gastric bypass surgery. He was referred for psychological assessment to determine his readiness for the surgery. The psychologist prepared a report that was sent to his surgeon and reviewed by a nurse on the surgical team. It will remain in his medical record. Although Juan and his future treatment providers could access the report, it is unlikely that they will because it is specific to the surgical procedure. In this case, the primary audience is the surgical team, and secondary audiences are unlikely. The report should be directed to the surgical team. It could be argued that information that is not relevant to the decision about surgery should not be included in the report.

The key tasks in identifying the audiences for the report are the following:

• Define the primary audiences for the report by occupation and by relationship to the client. Write the report with these people in mind, imagining their needs and the language and concepts that will be most meaningful to them.

- Anticipate any secondary audiences for the report. Do not direct the report to these audiences, but include information that denotes the purpose of the assessment and its procedures, and make sure to use language and concepts in the report that are accessible to all.

Psychological assessment reports that are appropriately targeted to a primary audience, keeping in mind the likelihood of secondary audiences, are the most successful.

Client and Clinician Attributes

Client attributes are physical, emotional, motivational, attitudinal, or behavioral characteristics of the client that influence the course and outcomes of the interview, the administration of tests, and the interpretation of test results. Client attributes include barriers to communication, such as physical, cognitive, behavioral, or emotional limitations of the client (e.g., impaired vision or hearing, learning disabilities, low intellectual functioning, defiance, or high levels of anxiety), and language barriers. If there are barriers to communication or to the client's performance of required activities, it is essential for the psychologist conducting the assessment to take them into account when planning for the assessment and interpreting results. For instance, when Gregory, a 50-year-old deaf man who was hospitalized following a suicide attempt, was referred for assessment to clarify his diagnosis, a sign language interpreter was made available to the psychologist conducting the assessment. Deafness affected Gregory's performance on the verbal subtests of the WAIS-III and made it impossible to complete certain projective tests even with the help of the interpreter. The use of an interpreter also had an impact on the clinical interview.

Gender and age can also be important client attributes to consider. For example, Wanda, a college student, was struggling with the aftermath of a sexual trauma. She did not disclose her history of being raped to the young, male psychologist conducting an assessment for learning problems and anxiety; but a few months later, she spoke about it at length to a female psychologist at the counseling center.

Less obvious but equally relevant client attributes include the client's motivation for the assessment, possible ramifications of the assessment for the client, and the client's understanding of those ramifications. Is the client nervous because he has performance anxiety or because the results of the assessment bear on something that is highly important to him? Is she withholding information because she is paranoid or because disclosure could result in serious problems? Interpreting assessment results without knowledge of these client attributes is misguided, ineffective, and unethical at best, and could cause the client harm.

A client's previous personal experiences with assessment, or experiences that other people have had that he has heard about, are also important factors to consider. For example, a child may have heard from a peer that children are tested when they are getting ready to go to a residential program. When he finds out he is being tested, he thinks he is being placed too, and he may appear to be highly anxious and depressed when otherwise he would not be.

Cultural factors are also important client attributes to consider. If the question is, Is Johnny depressed? and Johnny emigrated to the United States from China a few years earlier, it is essential to know what depression might look like in a recent Chinese immigrant. Is his reticence in talking about himself a sign of withdrawal or of deference to authority? The cultural, racial, or ethnic background of a client, and his or her identification with that background (as opposed to having assimilated mainstream Western, middle-class values), affects his or her interactions with the psychologist, presentation of signs and symptoms of mental disorders, display of emotions, other interpersonal behaviors, personality characteristics, sense of self, and responses to test items, at the least. Psychologists must be both thoughtful and culturally competent in assessing clients of diverse backgrounds. Among other things, the psychologist conducting the assessment must always consider whether the normative data used in the development of a specific test are relevant to the client.

In addition, psychologists must always be aware that even the most stable and well prepared among us come to the task of assessment with all kinds of biases, stereotypes, anxieties, personal problems, and limits to our knowledge and experience. The use of standardized tests is helpful in overcoming these limitations, but tests do not take the place of self-awareness, cultural competence, and an open mind.

The key issues to consider in regard to client and clinician attributes are as follows:

- Are there any barriers to the client's full participation in the assessment process?
- What is the client's attitude about the assessment, and why does he or she hold that attitude?
- What are the possible consequences of the assessment findings for the client?
- What are the cultural factors that need to be taken into account in planning the assessment and interpreting the results?
- What biases, stereotypes, anxieties, or personal problems do you, as the clinician, bring to the assessment, and how will you handle them?
- Do you, the clinician, need a better knowledge base to complete the assessment, and if so, how are you going to obtain it?

Systems Issues

It is common for clients to be referred for assessment by someone who works for a larger system, such as a public school, a hospital, or the judicial system. The client is often involved in the system at many levels, and the assessment is one piece of a much bigger picture. It is essential to determine how the assessment fits into the bigger picture for the client, and it is not possible to make this determination without some understanding of how the "pieces" of the system work. System factors also play a large part in determining the resources that can be brought to bear on a problem, and thus they affect the kinds of recommendations that are going to be of practical value.

For example, when Patrick, a 16-year-old high school student with regular attendance habits, refused to participate in class or do any homework, he was referred for assessment to determine if the school needed to make accommodations to support his learning. This question could not be addressed if the examiner did not know under what circumstances the school was required to provide accommodations or what accommodations might be available. Similarly, when Jonah, a 9-year-old, was arrested for setting off fireworks in front of his school at recess, a juvenile court judge ordered an assessment to assist in the disposition of his case. If the psychologist had not been familiar with the court system and did not know what could happen in Jonah's case, he would not have been able to complete the assessment.

Each system that regularly makes use of psychological assessment has its own language, rules, and expectations. These affect how the psychologist enters the system, who she interacts with, communication patterns, the topics that will be addressed and emphasized in the final report, and the language and content of the report. The 9-year-old boy mentioned above, Jonah, might be referred through school, the courts, a psychiatric hospital, his attorney, or his parents. Each referral would proceed differently, although, substantively, the findings and recommendations flowing from the assessment should be similar.

How does a psychologist new to a system find out how it works? The psychologist needs to find a way to fit into the system, adapting to its needs, so that the assessment process is comfortable and smooth as well as effective. Careful observation, study of relevant systems issues, such as special education regulations, consultation with other psychologists, and identification of staff who can answer questions are all essential to success, as is respect and consideration for those responsible for the everyday work in a system, such as members of a treatment team. Also, it is not unusual for a client to be involved with more than one system, often in an integrated fashion. For example, an inpatient in a psychiatric hospital might be referred for assessment, but he will be discharged to an outpatient clinic and case management, and when making recommendations the psychologist will need to have a good understanding of those systems as well.

Thus, it is important for the psychologist conducting the assessment to:

- be able to describe the system in which the assessment takes place,
- know the legal regulations as well as standards of practice in the system,
- know what is expected of the assessment and of the assessor, and
- identify personnel who can answer questions.

How Do These Factors Frame the Report?

The above five factors inform every aspect of an effective assessment. They inform the psychologist about the data that need to be gathered to answer referral questions as well as how to gather it, the conclusions to draw from it, and how to write the report. They help the psychologist determine what the client will respond best to and what to avoid, and they help the psychologist prepare a persuasive and effective report. In addition, an understanding of client attributes informs the psychologist about how to interpret the data, and an understanding of systems issues alerts the psychologist to what the report should contain in order to meet expectations and requirements.

An analysis of these five factors is achievable, even for the novice, but it takes some time and, even more important, careful attention. The checklist presented in the appendix may be used to ensure that you complete a thorough review of the contextual factors relevant to each assessment client.

APPENDIX: CONTEXT WORKSHEET

Initiation and funding

Who made the referral? _____

Occupation/role (e.g., parent): _____

Organization (if applicable): _____

Knowledge about assessment/experience with assessment:

_____

_____

_____

_____

Who is paying for the assessment? _____

Audience for the findings

Primary audience(s): _____

Possible secondary audience(s): _____

Explicit and implicit referral questions

Anticipated functions of the report:

_____

_____

_____

Explicit questions:

_____

_____

_____

_____

_____

Implicit questions:

_____

_____

_____

_____

_____

(Continued)

Client attributes

Barriers to participation:

_____

_____

_____

_____

_____

Attitude about participation:

_____

_____

_____

_____

Relevant cultural issues:

_____

_____

Clinician attributes

Anticipated challenges?

_____

_____

_____

_____

Feelings and thoughts about the assessment?

_____

_____

_____

_____

_____

Level of confidence:

_____

_____

_____

Degree of anxiety:

_____

_____

_____

Need to learn more? _____

How will you go about it?

_____

_____

_____

_____

Systems issues

What are the relevant systems involved with the referred client?

_____

_____

_____

_____

How do they relate to each other?

_____

_____

_____

_____

How will systems issues affect the assessment?

_____

_____

_____

_____

CHAPTER 3

Gathering Information

The Functions of Information

Information serves a number of purposes in psychological assessment. An IQ score, a Minnesota Multiphasic Personality Inventory-2 (MMPI-2) profile, facts about the structure of a family, a developmental history, and innumerable other data points provide the information a clinician needs to do her work. Typically, the clinician analyzes the data she gathers to answer referral questions, such as, "Is Marco depressed?" or "Does Malia have a learning disability?" However, in some situations, the clinician gathers information for other people to analyze; she measures attributes and describes the findings.

In addition to directly addressing referral questions or providing data, information allows the clinician to describe clients and to develop narratives, or tell stories, about them. The "story" frames the answers to referral questions and helps the reader know the person in question. It also helps the clinician prepare an interesting, readable report. Information also builds the credibility and persuasiveness of the clinician. Although a detective can solve a mystery by simply naming the perpetrator of a crime, the solution becomes more believable when he gives facts that build on each other to establish a solid case. Likewise, the data points a clinician gathers are used to build a case for her conclusions, both for the clinician herself and for her audience.

Most psychologists conducting assessments rely on more than one source of information. In an assessment of this type—often called multimethod assessment—information is derived from a number of sources; for example, projective and self-report measures, an interview of the client, and an interview with a family member. For many clinicians, multimethod assessment is the best means of sorting out clinical problems. According to Meyer et al. (2001),

> Under optimal conditions, (a) unstructured interviews elicit information relevant to thematic life narratives, though they are constrained by the range of topics considered and ambiguities inherent when interpreting this information; (b) structured interviews and self-report instruments elicit details concerning patients' conscious understanding of themselves and overtly experienced symptomatology, though they are limited by the patients' motivation to communicate

frankly and their ability to make accurate judgments; (c) performance-based personality tests (e.g., Rorschach, TAT) elicit data about behavior in unstructured settings or implicit dynamics and underlying templates of perception and motivation, though they are constrained by task engagement and the nature of the stimulus materials; (d) performance-based cognitive tasks elicit findings about problem solving and functional capacities, though they are limited by motivation, task engagement, and setting; and (e) observer rating scales elicit an informant's perception of the patient, though they are constrained by the parameters of a particular type of relationship (e.g., spouse, coworker, therapist) and the setting in which the observations transpire. *These distinctions provide each method with particular strengths for measuring certain qualities* [italics added], as well as inherent restrictions for measuring the full scope of human functioning. (p. 145)

No single tool in the psychologist's toolbox is flawless. Each method has its strengths and limitations, and the information it provides contributes, sometimes more, sometimes less, to the clinician's efforts to understand a client and her problems.

In marked contrast to the generally positive point of view about the advantages of multimethod assessment of Meyer et al. (2001), Hunsley and Meyer (2003), in one of a series of articles about incremental validity, raise the question of whether adding assessment data from different instruments and sources improves clinical decisions and outcomes. Incremental validity is specifically concerned with whether a measure adds "to the prediction of a criterion above what can be predicted with other sources of data" (p. 446). According to these authors, despite the prevalence of multimethod assessment and the logic behind it, the advantage of adding measures to improving outcomes or making better decisions has yet to be proven. Nevertheless, assessment of children and adults almost always involves multiple methods and even those calling for more research on incremental validity and utility acknowledge "that the rationale supporting the use of . . . multiple measures is strong" (Johnston & Murray, 2003, p. 501).

This bit of controversy about the value of multimethod assessment points to the importance of carefully thinking through what information should be gathered to address the questions posed in an individual assessment case. There is little empirical evidence to provide guidance. Use common sense. Assessment is time-consuming and expensive, and it is demanding for the client as well as the clinician. In most cases, a combination of methods is preferable to a single method, but when choosing multiple methods to assess a particular client, there may come a point when additional tests no longer provide additional information.

Challenges in Gathering Information

The information that a clinician gathers to address referral questions concerns the behavior and personality of an individual, including his cognitive, emotional, and/or social functioning. However, people are not easily measured. The constructs that clinicians use to describe people are not well-defined, and there is not always agreement among psychologists about those constructs that are relevant to describing human behavior. Thus, a clinician conducting psychological assessments must gather information without being certain about what information is relevant or how to accurately measure it. In addition, there are limitations to clinical judgment and limitations to tests and techniques that make psychological assessment especially difficult.

Limitations of the Clinician

Even the best clinicians are limited by their ignorance, bias, and imperfect reasoning skills. Furthermore, clinicians are subject to a number of problems in thinking that interfere with good clinical judgment, and research on the matter indicates that experience does not improve clinical judgment (see Garb, 1998). In his text on clinical judgment, Garb (1998) convincingly notes that clinicians engage in confirmatory bias. They seek information that confirms their hypotheses, giving their initial, subjective impressions about a client more credence than they merit. Also, clinical judgment relies on implicit theories of personality and psychopathology, and these are not always correct. One specific problem is that clinicians tend to compare clients with clinical prototypes that are grounded in clinical experience, not in empirical research. For example, a clinician may have had a client, Joan, who did not remember being sexually abused in childhood. Joan behaved like many of the clinician's other clients who had a history of sexual abuse. Later, Joan recalled being abused, and the abuse was confirmed by family members. The clinician is likely to be swayed more by this powerful clinical experience than by the findings of research studies that indicate that there is no correlation between behavior patterns in adulthood and repressed memories of sexual abuse.

Of course, relying too heavily on hard evidence can also lead to errors. In special education, for example, until recently psychologists relied on mathematical formulas to determine the presence of learning disabilities, undoubtedly missing the diagnosis of learning disabilities in many youngsters who had brain-based reading disorders and other learning problems. However, clinical judgment research suggests that relying only on clinical judgment (for example, making a diagnosis of a reading disability based on observing that Jane does not read as fluently as her peers and reverses letters when she writes, problems often found in students who have reading disorders) is likely to produce even more errors.

The essential challenge of psychological assessment is to draw accurate and meaningful conclusions about a client, to minimize false positives and false negatives, to be "right"—to recognize depression in a client who has depression or a reading disability and attention-deficit/hyperactivity disorder (ADHD) in a client who has both of these conditions, or not diagnosing a client who in fact doesn't qualify for a diagnosis. Unfortunately, relying on clinical judgment too often leads the clinician toward erroneous conclusions.

Garb (1998) made a number of practical suggestions to minimize the risks of drawing incorrect conclusions based on clinical judgment, including the following:

- Keep in mind that relying on clinical experience is likely to lead to less accurate judgments than relying on empirical research. What does the research literature tell us, for example, about the behaviors of adults who were sexually abused as children? What does it tell us about the implications of letter reversals in 8-year-olds or the accuracy of computerized tests of attention in diagnosing ADHD?

• Consider alternative explanations of behaviors, especially cultural or situational factors. Is a child wearing her shirt inside out because of inattentiveness, or is this the style among her peers?

• Memory is vulnerable to distortion, so carefully document observations and review notes prior to drawing any conclusions.

• Make a significant effort to become aware of one's own personal biases and stereotypes and overcome them.

These suggestions are reasonable and clinicians have no good reason not to carry them out.

Limitations of Tests and Techniques

Using well-validated, reliable psychological tests and techniques that have appropriate normative data provides a partial solution to the problem of clinical judgment, but psychological tests are imperfect. Tests may not be reliable, valid, or relevant in a given situation. They may not tell the clinician what she needs to know to answer referral questions. They may provide distorted or inadequate data. Furthermore, even when computer scored and interpreted, tests are ultimately used by clinicians in drawing conclusions about clients. For example, a mother completes a Conners' Parent Rating Scale-Revised (CPRS-R) form for her 14-year-old son. None of the scales are elevated, suggesting that ADHD is not a clinically significant problem. Yet the boy, in every other respect, appears to be struggling with symptoms of ADHD. What should the clinician make of the mother's CPRS? Perhaps the boy is not hyperactive at home, but he is hyperactive at school and in the neighborhood. Perhaps she is inattentive herself, or she has an unusually high threshold for hyperactive behavior. Maybe she is comparing him with his younger brother, who is even more hyperactive. Although the CPRS has excellent empirical support, it is the clinician who gives meaning to the findings. As Conners (2003) points out in the CPRS-R manual,

> Paper-and-pencil ratings are subject to their own biases and the subjectivity of the rater. . . . Use of the information must include a clinical judgment about the relative quality of the data sources and the reason for any reported discrepancies. (p. 46)

Another common problem is that a well-validated test may not be appropriate for a client or for the assessment situation. For example, although the Minnesota Multiphasic Personality Inventory-Adolescent form (MMPI-A) is a well-validated test, the reading level may be too high for some teenagers who might otherwise benefit from it, or it may take too long to administer in some assessment situations. Furthermore, language and other barriers to testing, or inadequate normative data, may make otherwise good tests unusable or invalid for specific clients.

In addition, there may not be well-validated tests available to provide needed information in every situation. For example, there may not be a well-validated test that can assess strengths and deficits in a client who lacks self-awareness or is unwilling to acknowledge problem areas. The Brown ADD Scales (Brown, 1996) get around this problem by using both the client and an informant to provide information about a client's behavior. Although the informant's ratings are not scored, they are a useful and necessary adjunct, especially when a client denies behaving in problematic ways. Perhaps clinicians continue to use controversial projective techniques, such as the Rorschach, for just this reason. They assess a range of characteristics relevant to emotional and behavioral functioning that cannot be assessed with other available techniques.

Finally, test results can give the clinician a false sense of security. Psychological tests are administered and scored (or data are entered into a computer for scoring) by people, and people are prone to error. It is very easy to make a mistake and not recognize it; for example, to make an addition error in scoring a Wechsler Intelligence Scale for Children-Fourth Edition (WISC-IV) subtest, resulting in a scaled score of "6" (below average) rather than "8" (average). Clearly, tests have to be administered, scored, and interpreted correctly for results to be meaningful. It is tempting to "hang one's hat" on numbers, since they seem so sturdy and scientific. However, if a psychologist administers a WISC-IV, the Woodcock-Johnson Tests of Cognitive Abilities III (WJC), and the Woodcock-Johnson Tests of Achievement III (WJA) to a child, he obtains well over 30 test scores and summaries of test scores, but the scores don't mean anything until the psychologist determines their reliability and makes sense of them in relationship to the child's behavior and situation.

Steps in Gathering Information

Despite the numerous challenges to gathering information, psychologists routinely conduct worthwhile, valuable assessments that answer a wide range of questions about people and their problems. How do they do it? They understand the context of the assessment and are cognizant of the limitations of clinical judgment and of psychological tests. They decide what information they need to understand a problem and to convince their audience that their conclusions are correct. They interview the client and sometimes informants, review records, administer tests, and revise their assessment plan as they go forward. We offer the following steps to gathering information as a guide.

Identify the Referral Questions

Referral questions are the starting point in gathering information. Does a child have a reading disability? Does a young adult have schizophrenia? What is the best way to manage an elderly person's suicidal risk? Defining the relevant questions guides the psychologist in choosing what information to gather and how to gather it.

Chapter 2, on understanding the context of the assessment, offers explicit instructions on how to go about identifying explicit and implicit referral questions. The questions are needed at this stage to formulate an assessment plan.

Learn About the Problem

One of the challenges in being a new clinician is that there is so much to learn. To conduct an effective assessment, the clinician needs information about the problem under consideration, whether it's a question of a reading disability or psychosis. For assessments that serve clinical or educational functions, the clinician needs to make sure she knows how the problem is typically manifested, that is, its signs and symptoms, and what types of interventions might be available and helpful. For assessments that serve gatekeeping or administrative functions, the clinician must know the criteria used in decision making, for example, the criteria used to determine eligibility for academic accommodations. We recommend both study and supervision to learn about the problems to be addressed in the assessment. Both have their place, and they complement each other well.

Review Records

At this stage, it is a good idea to review any records about the client that are available. School records, psychological testing reports, educational evaluations, medical or hospital records, legal reports, and many other kinds of records are frequently made available to clinicians conducting psychological assessments. However, it is important to recognize that information contained in records was gathered for purposes other than the current assessment. It may or may not be accurate or relevant.

A review of records usually contributes to an understanding of the context of the assessment. It also delineates specific events or detailed information that the clinician conducting the assessment might not otherwise be aware of. For example, a medical record might note that the client made a suicide attempt at some point in the past or that she tried a number of different antidepressants without success. A school record could indicate that a student had multiple disciplinary problems and once went through an expulsion hearing. Such facts often need to be taken into account when making recommendations for a client.

Information contained in records can also contribute directly to answering referral questions. For example, in making a differential diagnosis between a mood disorder and schizophrenia, it can be helpful to look at hospital records to trace the course of illness. Similarly, in making a diagnosis of a learning disability, it is important to review a student's performance through the grades.

It is essential to keep in mind that the information contained in records, unless it is obviously factual, might not be accurate. It is best to confirm information with the client through the interview process if it will be included in the report and if there are any doubts about its veracity. A report that contains inaccurate information loses credibility.

Identify the Domains of Functioning That Need to Be Assessed

Sorting behavior, experience, attitudes, and ideas into domains or areas is a useful method of organizing one's thinking about them. Behavior, experience, and so forth can be categorized in any number of ways. For example, Walsh (2007) assesses the domains of behavioral, emotional, and educational outcomes in her study of adolescent resilience. Lombardo (2003) evaluates quality of life in cancer patients by looking at domains of physical, emotional, social, functional, and overall well-being. The World Health Organization (WHO) in its International Classification of Functioning, Disability, and Health (ICF) classifies problems related to disability in terms of mental functions, breaking these down to include consciousness, memory, intellect, emotions, personality, and several others (WHO, 2001, chap. 1). Brown, Myers, Mott, and Vik (1994) evaluate the psychosocial functioning of teenagers after substance abuse treatment by examining domains of school functioning, interpersonal problems, emotional problems, family functioning, and number of activities. From a psychoanalytic perspective, Schneider and several colleagues (2002) propose an alternative to the *DSM-IV* categorization of mental disorders based in part on assessment of the following domains: self-perception, self-regulation, defenses, object perception, communication, and attachment. As is evident from the wide range of domains of functioning captured in the above descriptions, categorization of human behavior into domains of functioning is guided by theoretical orientation and task requirements. Part of the job of a psychologist conducting an assessment is to choose which domains of functioning to assess. It is only important that the choice is theoretically or empirically grounded and relevant to the purpose of the assessment.

For a child referred to a school psychologist to evaluate his cognitive abilities in preparation for determining his eligibility for special education services, it is obvious that the domain of functioning that needs to be assessed is intellectual. An adult referred for differential diagnosis of schizophrenia and bipolar disorder will need an assessment of the domains of thought and mood problems. An aggressive adolescent referred for treatment recommendations might need an assessment of these domains, at a minimum: intellectual and emotional functioning, personality characteristics, coping skills, and situational factors that precipitate or prevent outbursts.

Psychologists conducting assessments can, in most circumstances, choose domains that are relevant to the assessment from the following list:

- Emotional functioning
- Intellectual functioning
- Memory and executive functions
- Academic achievement
- Behavior
- Interpersonal relationships
- Thought processes
- Self-concept

- Family functioning
- Family history
- Situational stress
- Symptoms (of specific psychiatric disorder)

Thus, for a treatment-oriented assessment of a school-avoidant 10-year-old, the clinician might assess family functioning, situational stress, symptoms of anxiety or depression, learning problems, behavior problems, interpersonal relationships, and self-concept. Note that assessment in some of these domains might be brief and informal, so it's not as daunting a task as it might seem.

Sidebar 3.1

Selecting Tests

A Process for Selecting Tests

Determine the reason for referral and the domains of functioning that need to be assessed → select and administer tests → revise the referral questions and domains → select and administer additional tests

A Checklist for Selecting Tests

Is the test valid and reliable?

Does it have extensive and appropriate normative data?

Does it provide information about the domains of functioning relevant to the referral question?

Is it cost-effective in terms of money and time?

Does it provide unique information?

Is it culturally, developmentally, and cognitively appropriate for the client?

Does it meet the expectations of the agency or individual making the referral?

Select Tests and Other Assessment Procedures

There are hundreds of psychological and educational tests available to psychologists conducting assessments. How should the psychologist choose among them? The selected tests must be valid and reliable, and in most cases they should have extensive and appropriate normative data. They should offer information about the domains of functioning relevant to the referral question. They should be cost-effective; that is, they should provide maximum information in the minimum time and with minimum labor. They should provide unique information. They should be culturally, developmentally, and cognitively appropriate for the client. Finally, they should meet the expectations of the agency or individual making the referral.

Selecting tests for assessment is an iterative process, going something like this: determine the reason for referral and the domains of functioning that need to be assessed, select and administer tests, adjust the referral questions and domains, and select and administer additional tests. Chapters 4 to 6 review tests that provide information across a variety of domains and are a good starting point to putting together a test battery, keeping in mind the criteria described above.

Administer, Score, and Interpret Tests

The key to success in administering, scoring, and interpreting psychological tests, especially for new clinicians, is simple: follow instructions in the test manual. Following standardized procedures is the best assurance of valid results. To meet that goal, the examiner must be familiar and comfortable with administering whatever tests are selected. He should review and practice procedures of unfamiliar tests in advance of administering them. Deviations from standardized procedures may be necessary from time to time, but these should be noted in the report, and an estimate of the impact of the deviation must also be recorded.

When administering tests, the examiner should record observations about the client. These observations are behavioral referents. They help answer referral questions and, among other things, guide the clinician in determining if the assessment plan needs to be revised. Observations made during test administration also contribute to the examiner's judgment about the validity of test results. Perhaps the client is nervous or easily distracted, tired, or preoccupied. These behaviors can make test results inaccurate to a mild extent or more significantly. The examiner needs to make a judgment about the impact of behavior on test findings.

When scoring tests, it is essential to remain objective and to be accurate. Score the protocol twice if necessary, to make sure that there are no mistakes. Follow directions in the test manual precisely, because loosely interpreting instructions can invalidate results. A common mistake is to give a client the benefit of the doubt when deciding how to score an item. This can lead to problems such as overestimating cognitive ability or underestimating problem areas. When uncertain about how to score an item, review the scoring decision with a colleague or supervisor.

When interpreting test results, follow instructions from the test manual and from guidebooks specific to the test. Interpret results at a level appropriate to the context of the assessment. If the referral is from a psychoanalytic therapist and the purpose is to gain insight about a client's dynamics and their impact on treatment, deep levels of interpretation that require a high level of inference are appropriate. The clinician should also be well trained in providing them. If the purpose of the assessment is to recommend a type of treatment or program, a lower level of inference and interpretations that are closer to the data are called for. Computer-assisted interpretation is absolutely appropriate, but it is essential for the psychologist to know whether the interpretive report is based on actuarial or clinical evidence and to use good judgment in accepting the interpretations. Just as interpretations from a test manual should be thoughtfully considered, computer-assisted interpretations should not be taken indiscriminately.

Test interpretation, especially the integration of the results of multiple tests, incorporates art as well as science. When it is primarily art—that is, when there is no "cookbook" or actuarial data to guide interpretation—the inexperienced clinician should be closely supervised to avoid "wild analysis," interpretations that stray too far from the data.

Determining Reliability, Validity, and Usefulness of the Data

All the data are collected, but the task of gathering information is not complete until the quality of the gathered information is determined. It is a mistake to draw conclusions from data that are unreliable or invalid, and it is not sensible to draw conclusions from data that are not relevant to referral questions.

How are the reliability and validity of the data determined? A reliable test is one in which results are consistent from day to day or examiner to examiner. A valid test is one that measures what it is supposed to measure. Is the client tearful and agitated because of an unusual event that just occurred or due to an underlying mental illness? Did she score poorly on cognitive testing because she had a really bad cold that day? Is he malingering, that is, faking, psychotic symptoms during the interview? It is the clinician's responsibility to determine if the data he collected are reliable and valid before using the data to draw conclusions about his client.

It is relatively easy to obtain reliable and valid data, but reliable and valid data may not have relevance to the referral questions under consideration. For example, an MMPI-2 profile might be reliable and valid, but it won't provide any information about whether a client has a learning disability. The client's history of growing up in a family in which there was a great deal of alcoholism, discovered in the clinical interview, might be interesting but irrelevant to the question of whether he has an underlying thought disorder.

The question of usefulness is broader. Useful data can inform recommendations or paint a descriptive picture of a client, even when it is not directly relevant to referral questions. Knowing that the client being evaluated for thought disorder grew up in a family affected by alcoholism allows the reader to form a fuller understanding of the client and his problems, to see him more clearly as an individual. The information may be useful in planning treatment, preventing alcohol dependence, or helping a therapist develop a relationship with the client.

Case Example

Dr. Velez was hired by a local school district to evaluate a third-grade student, Eva, who attended a charter school. She displayed significant behavior problems in the classroom, and these were spilling over into her academic work which was becoming increasingly inadequate. Dr. Velez was asked to assess Eva's intellectual functioning and level of academic achievement, to rule out learning disabilities, attention problems, or other processing problems. She was also asked to make recommendations about managing Eva's behavior in the classroom. Based on her knowledge of behavior problems in children, Dr. Velez determined that she needed to assess the following domains of functioning: cognitive ability; academic achievement in reading, writing, and math; attentional capacities; impulse control; behavioral, emotional, and interpersonal functioning; and family problems. She made the following assessment plan:

Review school records

Interview child

Interview mother

Interview classroom teacher

Interview another teacher

Classroom observations (at least two)

WISC-IV (cognitive ability, attentional capacity)

Woodcock-Johnson Tests of Achievement III (WJA) (rule out learning problems)

Rating Scales (Behavior Assessment System for Children-2 [BASC-2] series, Conners' Parent Rating Scale-Revised [CPRS-R])

Sentence completion, projective drawings (emotional functioning, self-concept)

Additional projectives as needed

Dr. Velez completed the assessment, first conducting interviews and observations, followed by the structured tests, and then the projectives. She found that Eva was experiencing a high level of anxiety related to family problems and a traumatic experience that took place at home the previous year. Her level of intellectual functioning was in the average range, but she showed signs of a reading disability, adding to her anxiety. Dr. Velez concluded that Eva's behavioral problems in the classroom were a manifestation of anxiety and also related to her undiagnosed reading disorder. Eva could not keep up with her classmates now that there were increasing demands for independent reading and learning from text. She recommended treatment for anxiety and special education services, and she made other specific recommendations to help Eva manage her behavior, keep up with her peers academically, and feel more comfortable in school.

4

Gathering Information

Measures of Intellectual, Academic, and Neuropsychological Functioning

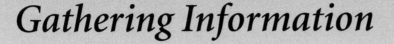

T his is the first of three chapters focusing on specific methods of gathering information during psychological assessment. In this chapter, we focus on measures of intellectual, academic, and neuropsychological functioning. In subsequent chapters, we turn our attention to measures of personality, measures of emotional and behavioral functioning, and clinical interviews. Throughout, we emphasize not only fundamental information about prominent techniques in each category but also real-world issues such as test selection and report writing.

Intelligence Tests

Tests of intelligence are used for a variety of purposes. In some assessments, intelligence is the primary, or only, component of the referral question. In others, such as learning disability assessments, intelligence is one of a small number of constructs measured. And in yet others, intelligence is one of many constructs measured, often providing contextual information when the main focus of the assessment is something other than intelligence. Regardless of purpose, intelligence tests measure a client's intellectual abilities, typically yielding an overall IQ score. "IQ," of course, stands for intelligence quotient, implying that intelligence is conceptualized as a ratio between intellect and age.

Defining Intelligence

Before we delve into particular tests of intelligence, it is important to consider how intelligence is defined, as well as the theories of intelligence that contribute to its definition. Actually, clinical psychologists have debated the definition of intelligence for as long as the field has existed. At different times and by different people, various capacities have been emphasized as central to intelligence, including processing speed, abstract thinking, problem solving, sensory capacity, capacity to learn from experience, ability to adapt to situational demands, reasoning, memory, and inhibition of impulse (e.g., Sternberg, 2000; Wasserman & Tulsky, 2005).

A particularly prominent conceptual debate among experts in the field of intelligence concerns the singular versus the plural nature of intelligence. That is, should we understand intelligence to be one thing, or many separate things? This debate was particularly active in the first half of the 1900s, when Charles Spearman argued that intelligence was singular. In fact, he used the term *g* to represent general, global, overall intellectual ability. He pointed to his own research, in which an individual's various specific abilities were likely to be correlated with each other, to support his argument. Louis Thurstone was among the leaders of the opposing side of this argument. Thurstone argued that each individual had numerous, separate intelligences that were not necessarily correlated with each other. According to his factor-analytic statistical methods, he concluded that an individual's abilities derived from multiple factors rather than a single one. In time, hierarchical models of intelligence emerged, which combined the notion of a general, overall intelligence with specific abilities that were at least somewhat related to it (Brody, 2000). A more recent variation of the hierarchical model is the three-stratum theory of intelligence (Carroll, 2005), in which there are three levels of ability, with more than 60 highly specific abilities contributing to 8 broad factors, which in turn contribute to 1 overall intellectual ability.

It is important to note that most of the intelligence tests used by assessors today—including those described in the subsequent sections—endorse a hierarchical model of intelligence, as evidenced by the scores they yield. The fact that they endorse the presence of a single, overall intelligence is reflected in the presence of a "full-scale" or "overall" IQ number. The fact that they also endorse more specific intellectual abilities is reflected in the presence of "index," "factor," or "subtest" scores. Knowledge of the theories or definitions of intelligence that underlie a particular intelligence test can enhance not only its interpretation but also its explanation in an assessment report.

Wechsler Intelligence Tests

Within clinical psychology, the Wechsler intelligence tests have earned a position of great respect, as indicated by a vast accumulation of supporting empirical research as well as by the popularity of the tests among assessors. David Wechsler published his first intelligence test, the Wechsler-Bellevue, in 1939. It was designed to measure the intelligence of adults, but as the years went by, Wechsler created an alternate test designed to measure the intelligence of school-age children, and eventually another to measure the intelligence of preschool children (Reisman, 1991). All these tests are revised periodically; today there are three current Wechsler intelligence tests in use: the Wechsler Adult Intelligence Scale-Third Edition (WAIS-III), published in 1997; the Wechsler Intelligence Scale for Children-Fourth Edition (WISC-IV), published in 2003; and the Wechsler Preschool and Primary Scale of Intelligence-Third Edition (WPPSI-III), published in 2002. A recent addition to the family of Wechsler intelligence tests, the WISC-IV Integrated, is notable. The WISC-IV Integrated, published in 2004, adds 16 additional subtests to those in the standard WISC-IV. The purpose of these subtests is to tap into processing issues that underlie a child's scores, knowledge of which may enhance suggestions or interventions. Most of these supplemental subtests involve tasks similar to the standard WISC-IV subtests, but with different methodologies, such as multiple choice rather than free recall items, or the removal of the opportunity for speed-based bonus points.

Although each of the Wechsler intelligence tests is customized for the age group it tests, the tests are all fundamentally similar in a number of important ways. For example, they all are individually administered and involve direct verbal interaction between the assessor and the client, unlike written tests that clients can take on their own. Each Wechsler test requires training to learn the proper administration technique as well as techniques of scoring and interpretation. Each features an average IQ score of 100, with a standard deviation of 15. Also, each Wechsler test includes 10 to 15 subtests, some of which are optional. These subtests involve both verbal and nonverbal tasks and are grouped together to form four separate index scores—(1) verbal comprehension, (2) perceptual reasoning, (3) working memory, and (4) processing speed—as well as a single, full-scale intelligence score. So the Wechsler tests provide a single, overall estimate of intelligence, estimates of four broad areas of intelligence, and estimates of 10 to 15 specific intellectual abilities. Chapter 8 includes segments of a sample report that features WISC-IV scores. Additionally, all three Wechsler intelligence tests are accompanied by large, carefully collected sets of normative data with which a client's raw scores are compared. And finally, the reliability and validity of the Wechsler tests are supported by a sizeable and growing body of psychometric data (see, e.g., Lichtenberger & Kaufman, 2004; Zhu & Weiss, 2005).

Especially in their most recent revisions, the Wechsler tests have reflected efforts toward increasing their cultural fairness and sensitivity. For school-age children, the Wechsler tests currently offer a fully Spanish intelligence test, the WISC-IV Spanish. The WISC-IV Spanish is administered in Spanish, and its items have been adapted from the original WISC-IV to reduce cultural bias. Its norms include populations from countries of origin that include Cuba, the Dominican Republic, and Puerto Rico; Mexico and other countries in Central America; and countries in South America. Non-English versions of other Wechsler intelligence tests may follow soon.

Stanford-Binet Intelligence Scales

The original editions of the Stanford-Binet actually predate Wechsler's first intelligence test. Its creators, including Alfred Binet, were called on by the French government to develop a test to identify public school students who needed special services from educators. The test they created to fill this need was the Binet-Simon scale, published in 1905, which was ultimately revised numerous times and renamed slightly, resulting in the current version of the test, the Stanford-Binet Intelligence Scales-Fifth Edition (SB5; Reisman, 1991).

Like the Wechsler tests, the Stanford-Binet tests have been highly respected and frequently used among clinical psychologists. In some ways, the current editions of the tests are quite similar; in others, they are quite distinct. Like the Wechsler tests, the SB5 incorporates a hierarchical model of intelligence. It uses many subtest scores to yield five "factor" scores as well as a single full-scale IQ score. Also like the Wechsler tests, the SB5 is administered interpersonally and requires training to use, and its reliability and validity are supported by a notable body of empirical research. A primary difference between the Stanford-Binet and the Wechsler tests is the fact that a single version of the Stanford-Binet test covers the entire life span beginning at age 2, whereas three different Wechsler tests target preschool, school-age, and adult clients. The subtests of the SB5 also include more items at the low and high ends of difficulty, which can be helpful in assessing clients at the extreme ends of intelligence during assessments of mental retardation or giftedness. Additionally, the specific subtests and five factors—(1) fluid reasoning, (2) knowledge, (3) quantitative reasoning, (4) visual-spatial processing, and (5) working memory—measured by the SB5 differ from those measured by the Wechsler tests (Kamphaus & Kroncke, 2004).

Other Tests of Intelligence

Although the Wechsler and Stanford-Binet tests have been prominent, there are many additional options for assessing intelligence. For example, the Kaufman Assessment Battery for Children–Second Edition (KABC-II) is an alternative to the WPPSI-III and the WISC-IV; the Kaufman Brief Intelligence Test–Second Edition (KBIT-II) offers a brief (approximately 20 minute) way to measure verbal and non-verbal intelligence in child and adult clients. The Woodcock-Johnson III NU Complete includes two full batteries (one to measure intelligence, the other to measure achievement) co-normed on the same sample; this test is frequently used in learning disability assessments. A Spanish adaptation of the Woodcock-Johnson, the Batería III Woodcock-Muñoz, assesses intelligence and achievement of Spanish-speaking clients across the life span.

Some tests of intellectual ability are less comprehensive, including the Peabody Picture Vocabulary Test-IV (PPVT-IV), in which each item involves the assessor stating one word and presenting four drawings to the client. The client's task is to choose the drawing that corresponds to the word stated by the assessor. Responses indicate receptive vocabulary and verbal skills, from which intelligence can be inferred. The Test de Vocabulario en Imagenes Peabody is a version of the PPVT in which the items have been translated into Spanish and the norms are based on scores of individuals of Mexican and Puerto Rican background.

The Wechsler, Stanford-Binet, and other popular tests of intelligence have often been criticized for including items that rely too heavily on verbal skills and culture-specific concepts, which can result in the intelligence of members of minority groups being underestimated. The Universal Nonverbal Intelligence Test (UNIT), originally published in 1996, exemplifies this effort to prevent aspects of culture from confounding the assessment of intelligence. The UNIT is an interpersonally administered test, but it does not rely on spoken language at all. Instead, the assessor's instructions occur in the form of hand gestures, and the client's responses involve only pointing or manual manipulation of objects. The UNIT is for use only with school-age children, and it may not be as comprehensive as the more long-standing or widely accepted tests of intelligence; however, it offers psychologists a culturally sensitive option for the assessment of some culturally diverse clients (McCallum & Bracken, 2005).

Achievement Tests

In contrast to intelligence tests, which measure a client's intellectual abilities, achievement tests measure what a client has accomplished, especially in academic areas such as reading, math, or writing. A comparison of the results of a client's intelligence tests and achievement tests can indicate areas in which accomplishment falls short of ability. A significant discrepancy of this type is the basis of a learning disability diagnosis.

Wechsler Individual Achievement Test-Second Edition (WIAT-II)

The WIAT-II measures achievement in the areas of reading, math, written language, and oral language of clients age 4 to 85. Like most of the intelligence tests discussed above and most of the achievement tests discussed in this section, it is interpersonally administered rather than being a pencil-and-paper test that clients complete entirely on their own. In the WIAT-II, each of the four areas of achievement is represented by two to three subtests. For example, reading achievement is determined by the client's scores on three subtests: Word Reading, which involves reading single words aloud; Pseudoword Decoding, which involves sounding out nonsense words; and Reading Comprehension, which involves understanding the meaning of sentences or paragraphs. The WIAT-II produces scores that are directly comparable with Wechsler intelligence test scores to facilitate learning disability determination. It yields scores on the same scale as the Wechsler intelligence tests (mean of 100, standard deviation of 15) as well as grade and age equivalencies to help place test performance in a school context.

Wide Range Achievement Test-Fourth Edition (WRAT-4)

The WRAT-4 assesses achievement in word reading, spelling, math skills, and sentence comprehension. It is more time-efficient but less comprehensive than the WIAT-II described above. Each of the four areas is measured by only a single subtest. The WRAT-4 is often used in learning disability testing, but at times it is accompanied by more detailed testing of achievement in certain areas to substantiate a diagnosis.

Other Achievement Tests

The California Achievement Tests-Fifth Edition were originally designed by California school officials to measure skills of school-age children. Depending on the age of the child, the tests assess achievement in areas such as reading, language, spelling, mathematics, study skills, science, and social studies. Other comprehensive achievement tests include the Peabody Individual Achievement Test-Revised (Normative Update) and the Kaufman Test of Educational Achievement-Second Edition (KTEA-II), which, in its brief form, can assess achievement of clients across the life span in 15 to 45 minutes. Also, as mentioned in the previous section on tests of intelligence, the Woodcock-Johnson III NU Complete incorporates comprehensive tests of both achievement and intelligence, normed on the same population and suitable for learning disability testing.

Other achievement tests are less comprehensive but more exclusively focused in particular academic areas. For example, the KeyMath 3 focuses exclusively on achievement in mathematics, with 10 subtests covering the areas of computational skills, conceptual knowledge, and problem solving. The Gray Oral Reading Tests-Fourth Edition (GORT-IV), as the name indicates, focus solely on reading and provide information in areas such as reading rate, accuracy, fluency, and comprehension.

Neuropsychological Tests

Neuropsychological tests assess cognitive dysfunction or damage of the brain. Unlike medical tests such as CT and MRI scans, which can indicate that parts of the brain appear abnormal, neuropsychological tests indicate how parts of the brain function. Brief neuropsychological screens are often part of a more comprehensive assessment, while longer neuropsychological batteries are often used when the referral question involves a head injury, illness, or extensive substance use.

More than intelligence or achievement tests, neuropsychological tests require specialized training to administer, score, and interpret. Graduate programs in clinical psychology vary widely in the availability or requirement of training in neuropsychological testing, so merely earning a doctoral degree or becoming licensed as a psychologist does not qualify an assessor to conduct neuropsychological testing. Especially in the use of full neuropsychological batteries such as the Halstead-Reitan Neuropsychological Battery (HRB) and the Luria-Nebraska Neuropsychological Battery, special competencies must be obtained. These competencies are typically acquired in predoctoral or postdoctoral internships completed by individuals trained more generally in clinical psychology or a related field, and they are governed by specialty organizations such as the American Board of Clinical Neuropsychology and the American Board of Professional Neuropsychology. For these reasons, we focus in this chapter on brief neuropsychological screens, which require less expertise but yield less detailed results.

Before we consider specific examples of brief neuropsychological screens, it is important to make note of their limitations. Brief neuropsychological screens can alert the assessor to the likely presence of neuropsychological problems, but they can't offer much in terms of particulars. They are typically not adequate to localize problems to a particular lobe or region of the brain, and they are limited in their ability to specify which brain functions or mechanisms may be impaired. Often, the primary benefit of brief neuropsychological screens is their ability to suggest the need for further neuropsychological testing. In effect, they function much like the "Check Engine" light on a car's dashboard, in that they alert the assessor to the probable presence of problems.

Another clarification to make before describing specific neuropsychological tests is the relationship of such tests to tests of executive function. As the term implies, executive function involves the "execution" of mental tasks, and as such, it can affect planning, organizing, multitasking, sequencing, problem solving, attention, and memory. Although tests of executive function overlap with tests of other abilities such as memory and attention, there are some tests that have become closely identified with the assessment of executive function, such as the Wisconsin Card Sorting Test, the Trail Making Test, and the Stroop Color and Word Test. In recent years, tests specifically designed to assess executive function have emerged. For example, the Behavior Rating Inventory of Executive Functioning (BRIEF), published in 2000, is designed to assess executive functioning in individuals with neurological conditions such as traumatic brain injury, low birth weight, ADHD, developmental disorders, and learning disabilities. Although BRIEF was originally designed for school-age children, adult and preschool versions have also been developed.

Brief Neuropsychological Screens

In many psychological assessments, a brief neuropsychological screen is more appropriate than a full neuropsychological battery such as the Halstead-Reitan Neuropsychological Battery and the Luria-Nebraska Neuropsychological Battery. The Bender Visual-Motor Gestalt Test-Second Edition (Bender-Gestalt II) is a good example of such a screen; in fact, its first edition became the most common neuropsychological screen administered by clinical psychologists (Watkins, Campbell, Nieberding, & Hallmark, 1995), and the revision is similarly popular. The Bender-Gestalt II is a copying task in which the client uses pencil and paper to reproduce nine geometric designs consisting primarily of shapes, lines, dots, and angles. The client's task is to copy accurately, and inaccuracies, especially when they occur repeatedly in patterns, can indicate brain damage or other neuropsychological problems. Of course, brief screens such as the Bender-Gestalt II—which only takes about 6 minutes for clients to complete—can't localize brain damage or provide a detailed analysis of its consequences, but they can reflect problems in a more general sense and suggest the need for further neuropsychological testing (Lacks, 1999).

The Rey-Osterrieth Complex Figure Test is another neuropsychological screen used with some frequency in psychological assessments. Like the Bender-Gestalt II, it requires the client to use pencil and paper to copy, but it involves only a single, complex geometric figure. It also involves the use of pencils of different colors so that the assessor can trace the client's approach to copying the figure. Additionally, this test includes a memory-related task, in which clients are asked to draw the figure after they have copied it, and it has been removed (Helmes, 2000; Lacks, 2000).

Wechsler Memory Scale-Third Edition (WMS-III)

The Wechsler Memory Scale-Third Edition (WMS-III) is a commonly administered test in neuropsychological evaluations. It does not exactly belong in the same category as brief neuropsychological screens such as the Bender-Gestalt II or the Rey-Osterrieth Complex Figure Test due to its roughly half-hour length and focus on memory. However, it is not as lengthy or involved as full neuropsychological batteries such as the Halstead-Reitan Neuropsychological Battery or the Luria-Nebraska Neuropsychological Battery, and some graduate programs train students to use it.

The WMS-III assesses memory in adult clients via 11 subtests, 6 of which are mandatory and 5 of which are optional. It measures 8 "Primary Indexes" of memory, which includes visual, auditory, immediate, delayed, and working memory. It was co-normed with the WAIS-III, which facilitates comparisons of intelligence and memory-related abilities. Neuropsychological problems can be brought to light when this IQ/memory comparison reveals a significant discrepancy, as when memory scores fall below intelligence scores or when repeated administrations of the WMS-III indicate a decline in memory over time.

Factors to Consider in Selecting Tests of Intelligence, Achievement, and Neuropsychological Functioning

Assessors must give careful consideration to their choice of particular tests of intelligence, achievement, or neuropsychological functioning. Each referral question and each client is unique; this requires test selection to be customized. Of course, there are some fundamental criteria essential to the selection of any test, the most important of which are reliability and validity. Likewise, as the APA Ethical Code states, assessors should avoid tests that fall outside their boundaries of competence and tests that have become obsolete (APA, 2002). Ethical issues regarding assessment are covered in detail in Chapter 10. Here, we turn our attention to other important factors to be considered in test selection, particularly those that are most relevant to "real-world" assessment.

The Referral Question

Simply put, the referral question should guide test selection. The referral question not only suggests an overall category of testing, but it can suggest or rule out a particular type of test as well. For example, a referral for learning disability testing suggests that the use of intelligence and achievement tests are appropriate.

However, with additional information, test selection can be further customized. For example, if the client is a kindergarten student whose teacher has observed general struggles in learning, a comprehensive achievement test such as the WIAT-II might be most appropriate. However, if the client is a seventh grader struggling in math but not in other subjects, a specialized test such as the KeyMath 3, perhaps in addition to a more comprehensive achievement test, can be selected. Another example might involve an adult client who has experienced a head injury and has been referred for an evaluation of cognitive functioning. In general, a comprehensive IQ test such as the WAIS-III or SB5 is an appropriate choice. If the client has taken one of those tests previously, retesting with the same test might allow for even more meaningful pre- and postinjury comparisons. These examples highlight the importance for the assessor of attending to the referral questions. Moreover, they suggest that clarification of the referral question—asking for more information from the referral source about the reason behind it—can enhance test selection and, ultimately, the helpfulness of the information that the assessment results provide.

The Client's Culture and Language

Because a client's cultural background or linguistic abilities might influence the outcome of the assessment, assessors must be careful in selecting appropriate tests. As stated above, some long-standing, popular intelligence tests have been criticized for including items, especially on verbal subtests, that are difficult for members of minority cultures to answer. When a legitimate option—perhaps the UNIT, the PPVT-IV, or a translated version of a Wechsler test—is available, its use should be considered. When it is not, the results of the tests selected should be interpreted in the context of the client's belonging to a nonmainstream culture and language group. For example, if an assessor administers a neuropsychological battery in English and observes a client who struggles with English also struggling with some of the tasks involved in the battery, the assessor should consider the possibility that the directions may not have been fully understood, and may want to include a comment to that effect in the report.

In many cases, a full appreciation of the client's culture and language will require the assessor to inquire directly about these issues. In such cases, these questions should be considered a necessary part of the assessment process. Failing to obtain this information could result in false assumptions about the client's ability to speak a particular language or the client's ethnic background, which in turn could yield invalid assessment results.

The Client's Age

The age of the client is essential information for the selection of intelligence, achievement, and neuropsychological tests. In most cases, this is an uncomplicated issue: 5-year-olds take the WPPSI-III, 10-year-olds take the WISC-IV, and 40-year-olds take the WAIS-III. Difficult decisions for the assessor can arise, however, when a client's age falls near the boundary for a particular test. For example, at age 6, both the WPPSI-III and the WISC-IV are appropriate. Likewise, at age 16, both the WISC-IV and the WAIS-III are appropriate. In cases such as these, the assessor is obligated to have thorough knowledge of the manuals of the tests involved and other relevant data regarding test choice. Background information from which the assessor might infer the client's general level of intellectual functioning might guide the assessor to select the WAIS-III for a seemingly very bright 16-year-old but the WISC-IV for a 16-year-old whose intelligence is suspected to be much weaker.

Time Restrictions

Some referral questions come with firm, rapidly approaching deadlines. In such cases, lengthy tests or batteries such as the HRB or the WJ-III NU Complete may not be feasible to administer. Other tests, such as the KBIT-II for intelligence or the KTEA-II for achievement, may be better options. Of course, the assessor should never make claims about test results that can't be fully substantiated by the tests administered. In other words, if time restrictions prohibit the use of lengthier tests, but the briefer tests used in their place don't provide results as conclusive or detailed as the assessor had hoped, the assessor should not "stretch" the test results to provide an answer to the referral question. Similarly, there are limits on the extent to which an assessor can meet the time demands of the referral source. If a referral question comes along with a deadline that is simply unrealistic—that is, there is no way to select tests that would provide adequate information—the assessor can explain this problem to the referral source in the hope of gaining additional time. If this proves unsuccessful, the assessor should politely explain that such an assessment can't be completed in the allotted time rather than selecting tests that are too brief to suffice. For example, imagine that an assessor receives a call from a parent seeking measures of his or her child's IQ and achievement across all academic areas, along with a report detailing any learning disabilities uncovered by comparisons between the test results. If the parent can make the child available only for a single 2-hour appointment, the assessor simply cannot administer full-length tests such as the WISC-IV, the WIAT-II, or the WJ-III NU Complete in that time. The assessor might consider briefer tests, but might not feel comfortable attempting to definitively determine learning disabilities based on comparisons between a quick measure of IQ such as the KBIT-II and a quick measure of achievement such as the KTEA-II. In such a case, the assessor might choose to insist on more time or even to decline the assessment.

What to Include in the Assessment Report and How to Include It

Typically, results of intelligence, achievement, and neuropsychological tests are reported straightforwardly in psychological reports. In preparing these reports, however, assessors may encounter a number of "real-world" questions that require thoughtful responses.

How much background information should I include about each test? Assessors should not take for granted that the readers of their reports on intellectual, achievement, and neuropsychological measures—clients, parents, teachers, physicians, and others—are familiar with the assessment tests. The test names and acronyms that assessors know so well may be completely unfamiliar to the readers of the reports. Even the most intelligent readers might be ignorant of what "WAIS-III," "KeyMath," or "Bender-Gestalt" means if they have no training in psychological testing or the mental health field. For this reason, it can be a good idea to include in the report a brief explanation of a test the first time it is mentioned. For example, if an assessor is writing a report that will include results of the WISC-IV, introducing the results with a sentence such as "The WISC-IV is an intelligence test for children that covers a wide range of intellectual abilities" can familiarize the reader with the nature of the test. Likewise, if specific scores are listed, a statement such as "On the WISC-IV, mean scores for full-scale and index IQs are 100, and the mean score for each subtest is 10" can help to contextualize the numbers presented to the reader and make them more intelligible.

However, the assessor should also remember that the report is not a place for extensive background information about every test. Including too much can add unnecessary length to the report and take the focus away from the results. Thus, any background information about a particular test should be limited. Readers can seek additional information from other resources, including the assessor, if questions arise.

How should I organize the results of a particular test? Typically, when reporting the results of a particular test, it is best to begin with the broadest results first and subsequently report other findings in decreasing order of detail. Comparisons, both within a particular test and between tests, can be made after the results of the test are initially presented. For example, in an assessment that involves a Wechsler intelligence test, the full-scale IQ would be reported first, followed by the index scores, and then by the subtest scores. If some of these scores are to be compared with each other, or to scores from another test such as an achievement test, the comparisons typically appear after the scores are initially presented.

Should my report include specific test scores as opposed to summaries? Assessment reports about intelligence, achievement, and neuropsychological tests often include specific test scores. The other option, in which the assessor includes verbal summaries in place of the "numbers" produced by the report, is worthy of consideration if the reader of the report is likely to be confused by a series of actual test scores. Of course, such a verbal summary should be provided even if specific scores are reported; allowing the scores to stand alone and assuming that readers can make sense of them is a report-writing mistake.

Often, specific test scores are presented in a table rather than in the text to make them more intelligible. The organization of the table should reflect groupings or comparisons of scores that the assessor intends to make, and the text accompanying the table should offer relevant explanations.

Should I include percentiles or confidence intervals in my report? Manuals of tests of intelligence, achievement, and neuropsychological functioning frequently offer both percentile scores and confidence intervals to accompany particular scores. For example, on a Wechsler intelligence test, a full-scale IQ score of 103 represents the

58th percentile and falls within a confidence interval that extends several points above and below 103. The decision to include or exclude this information from the assessment report should be centered on its likely effect on the reader. Percentile scores can make individual test scores much more intelligible, especially for the nonprofessional report reader. Even if the report includes explanatory statements about average scores on particular tests or scales, percentile scores nonetheless translate scores to a familiar 100-point scale. Of course, if percentile scores are included, they should accompany rather than replace actual test scores. The possible inclusion of confidence intervals is a separate issue. On the one hand, including confidence intervals may remind the nonprofessional reader that tests of these types don't produce "pinpoint" results per se; in other words, without confidence intervals, some readers may mistakenly assume that the results are exact, rather than estimates. On the other hand, including confidence intervals can be confusing to some readers who don't understand the statistical reasoning behind them and can distract from the test scores themselves. Ultimately, the decision should be made on a case-by-case basis, but if confidence levels are included, like percentiles, they should accompany test scores rather than replace them.

To what extent should my report incorporate behavioral observations? Behavioral observations are an important part of any assessment, including an assessment of intelligence, achievement, or neuropsychological functioning. In fact, behavioral observations are part of what separates "testing" from "assessment." "Testing" suggests a series of scores presented with no context, whereas "assessment" places those scores in a context, a significant aspect of which consists of the behaviors exhibited by the client. Comments or questions offered by the client, behaviors suggesting depression or anxiety, signs of effort or lack thereof, and even attendance issues such as tardiness or a history of missing appointments can provide important information.

Behavioral observations can be drawn from any contact with the client, from the initial introduction to the final contact before the report is written. The assessor can observe and note in the report any relevant aspect of behavior, including physical features, such as appearance, hygiene, and bodily or facial features; attire, such as clothing, jewelry, makeup, and accessories; speech/thought process, such as organized or disorganized speech, coherence of thoughts, rate of speech; or mood/affect, such as facial expression, episodes of crying, voice inflection, and appropriateness of feelings to content of speech. And of course, bizarre or unusual behaviors are certainly noteworthy enough to merit inclusion in the report.

In many cases, behavioral observations can provide information relevant to validity of the test data itself. For example, if a 14-year-old child squints noticeably whenever faced with a visual task on the WIAT-II, it is possible that the results of those subtests and the WIAT-II in general are invalid. In other words, poor eyesight may restrict her ability to demonstrate her abilities, and her scores are therefore likely to be underestimates. Inclusion of this behavioral observation not only prevents an incorrect interpretation of the achievement test but may also lead to an important intervention in the form of a vision exam and possibly provision of glasses or contact lenses. As another example, consider a 45-year-old client taking the WAIS-III. The day before the appointment, his wife received news from her physician that she has a tumor, and it is not yet known whether the tumor is benign or cancerous. When he arrives at the testing, he mentions this to the assessor, and during the testing, he appears anxious. He bits his nails, taps his fingers on the table, and bounces his leg. He speaks hurriedly and frequently fails to pay attention. These behavioral observations are crucial to appreciating his WAIS-III scores, which may underestimate his true intelligence.

In other cases, behavioral observations may not reflect the validity or invalidity of test results as much as they provide context for the results, which increases understanding of the client. As another example, consider two 18-year-old clients who take the same intelligence test. They achieve identical scores, but one criticizes himself continuously throughout the testing, making comments such as "I should know that . . . ," "I'm so stupid . . . ," and "I'm sure I got that one wrong. . . ." The other appears aloof and disinterested, and the level of effort she puts forth appears inconsistent. In either case, reporting the client's scores without describing the context in which responses were produced tells only some of the story. Including the behavioral observations provides the opportunity for a more comprehensive, inclusive assessment of the client.

5

Gathering Information

Measures of Personality

In this chapter, we focus on the use of broad-based measures of personality in psychological assessment. By "broad-based," we refer to tests that yield scores on a wide range of personality traits or characteristics, as opposed to tests that focus more narrowly on one specific trait or characteristic. The tests discussed in this chapter tend to be longer and more comprehensive than such narrowly focused tests. As in the previous chapter on intellectual, academic, and neuropsychological functioning, our objectives are to present essential information about a variety of tests and to discuss "real-world" issues involved in their use by assessors.

Objective Personality Tests

Tests of personality are generally categorized as either objective or projective. Objective personality tests feature standardized, unambiguous test items, typically in the form of written statements or questions; a fixed range of responses from which clients may choose, such as multiple choices, true/false options, or Likert-scale ratings; and objective, uniform scoring methods. Usually, objective personality tests take the form of written questionnaires that clients read and to which they provide written responses. The items on these questionnaires are often statements or questions about the client's own behavior, feelings, tendencies, or preferences; thus, the method of data collection is self-report, as opposed to gathering information about a client via an informant. Projective personality tests, in contrast, involve intentionally ambiguous stimuli, a less limited range of client responses, and often an administration method that relies less on client reading and writing and more on interaction with the assessor. Specific projective personality tests will be covered in a subsequent section of this chapter. Here, we discuss numerous specific objective personality tests that are widely used among psychological assessors.

Minnesota Multiphasic Personality Inventory-Second Edition (MMPI-2)

The MMPI has a rich history within clinical psychology. The original version was published in 1943 as an attempt to objectively and empirically measure various types of psychopathology. Rather than relying solely on intuition or common sense to create questionnaire items that might bring forth different responses from normal and abnormal people as many previous questionnaire authors had, the MMPI authors created more than 1,000 such items, empirically tested them on normal and abnormal groups, and retained only those items that actually did bring forth different responses from members of different groups. The result was a list of 550 self-descriptive statements to which clients were instructed to respond "true" or "false."

A revision, the MMPI-2, was published in 1989. The format is identical to the original, and the length is similar. It is used to assess personality and psychopathology in adults age 18 and above. The norms of the revision are a much better representation of the current U.S. population than were the original norms, and the language included in the items is also more contemporary than the original.

The MMPI-2 yields scores on 10 clinical scales, each of which is designed to measure a particular type of psychopathology. The names of the 10 clinical scales indicate the various psychological problems assessed: hypochondriasis, depression, hysteria, psychopathic deviate (roughly equivalent to antisocial tendencies), masculinity-femininity, paranoia, psychasthenia (roughly equivalent to anxiety), schizophrenia, mania, and social introversion. Elevated scores on any of these clinical scales can be interpreted alone, but if there is more than one elevated score, they are typically interpreted in combination. (Although there is some variability between scales, in general, clinical scale t scores are considered moderately elevated when they are in the 60s, markedly elevated in the 70s and 80s, and extremely elevated at 90 or above.) In other words, assessors using the MMPI-2 often consider two- or three-scale code types when making sense of its results. Empirical research exists on interpretations of these two- and three-scale code types, offering clinical correlates of a variety of such combinations.

In addition to the 10 clinical scales, the MMPI-2 also features a large number of supplementary scales and content scales. These scales also focus on clinically relevant variables, but many do not correspond to particular diagnoses, and they tend to focus on more specific components of personality or psychopathology than the 10 clinical scales.

Besides these clinical, supplementary, and content scales, all of which provide clinical information, the MMPI-2 also yields validity scales. These validity scales assess the client's test-taking attitudes rather than personality or psychopathology. The MMPI-2 features three specific validity scales: L for lying in a "faking good" way; K for defensiveness, also suggesting "faking good"; and F for infrequency, suggesting "faking bad." Collectively, the validity scales inform the assessor about the client's approach to this self-report measure. That is, they allow the assessor to know if the client may have exaggerated or minimized his or her problems while responding to the test items, or if the client responded randomly without paying attention to each item. This information about the client's test-taking approach can supply important information regarding the interpretation of the clinical scales. For example, if the validity scales suggest that the client may have exaggerated his or her problems, elevated clinical scales may overestimate the severity of the client's pathology. In some cases, the validity scales suggest that the clinical profile is entirely invalid and should not be interpreted at all.

A tremendous body of empirical research supports the validity, reliability, and clinical use of the MMPI-2. In fact, it has been identified as the most psychometrically sound and widely used objective personality test (Butcher & Beutler, 2003; Camara et al., 2000; Frauenhoffer, Ross, Gfeller, Searight, & Piotrowski, 1998; Greene & Clopton, 2004). Besides the standard pencil-and-paper version, numerous formats of the MMPI-2 are available, including audio and computer-based formats. The MMPI-2 has also been translated into non-English languages, including Spanish, French, Hmong, and many others.

Minnesota Multiphasic Personality Inventory-Adolescent (MMPI-A)

In 1992, soon after the publication of the MMPI-2, another new version of the MMPI became available. As indicated by its name, the MMPI-A, with "A" standing for "adolescent," measures personality and psychopathology in clients age 14 to 18. The MMPI-A is quite similar to the MMPI-2. It shares the same true/false, self-report, pencil-and-paper format; it yields the same clinical and validity scales; elevated clinical-scale scores are defined similarly; and two- and three-point code types are typically interpreted similarly. It is slightly shorter in length, with 478 items. Some of its items are identical to those in the MMPI-2, while others are unique to the MMPI-A. The unique items focus on clinical issues prevalent among teenagers, such as drug and alcohol use, school-related problems, social problems with peers, and family relationships. The body of research specifically supporting the MMPI-A is not as massive as that supporting the MMPI-2, but those studies that have been conducted have reached similar conclusions about the reliability, validity, and clinical utility of the MMPI-A (Archer, 1997; Baer & Rinaldo, 2004). Like the MMPI-2, the MMPI-A has been translated into a wide variety of languages, including Spanish, French, and Korean.

Personality Assessment Inventory (PAI)

The PAI is a popular alternative to the MMPI-2. It also focuses on the assessment of psychopathology, with 11 clinical scales covering a wide range of psychological problems: somatic complaints, anxiety, anxiety-related disorders, depression, mania, paranoia, schizophrenia, borderline features, antisocial features, alcohol problems, and drug problems. It also includes five treatment scales intended to inform assessors and therapists about issues likely to be relevant to the treatment process as well as two interpersonal scales intended to measure social tendencies. Like the MMPI-2, it features validity scales that alert the assessor to inconsistencies among client responses, random/careless responding, faking bad, and faking good. The PAI was published in 1991, and is appropriate for clients age 18 and above. It is briefer than the MMPI-2, with 344 self-report items and a typical administration time of less than an hour. Each item offers four choices for client response: false, slightly true, mainly true, and very true (Morey, 2003). In addition to its original English version, the PAI is also available in a version translated into Spanish.

Millon Clinical Multiaxial Inventory-Third Edition (MCMI-III)

As the names of the clinical scales of the MMPI-2 and PAI indicate, they assess a broad range of psychopathology, including problems that appear on both Axis I and Axis II of the current edition of the *Diagnostic and Statistical Manual of Mental Disorders* (*DSM-IV*, American Psychiatric Association, 2000). In contrast, the MCMI-III emphasizes personality disorders (Axis II) over disorders appearing on Axis I. Its creator, Theodore Millon, is recognized as a leading scholar in personality disorders. In format, his measure is similar to the MMPI-2. It is a self-report, pencil-and-paper, true/false test. It contains only 175 items however, and its emphasis on personality disorders is evidenced by the fact that it yields scores on clinical scales corresponding to each of the 10 personality disorders included in the current *DSM*: antisocial, avoidant, borderline, dependent, histrionic, narcissistic, obsessive-compulsive, paranoid, schizoid, and schizotypal. Additionally, it yields scores on clinical scales corresponding to provisional personality disorders that may be included in future editions of the *DSM*: self-defeating, negativistic (passive-aggressive) and depressive. In addition to its clinical scales, the MCMI-III also yields modifier indices, which are similar to the validity scales of the MMPI-2 in that they assess the client's test-taking attitude. Psychometric data suggest that the reliability and the validity of the MCMI-III are strong (Meagher, Grossman, & Millon, 2004; Retzlaff & Dunn, 2003). The MCMI-III has been translated into Spanish and other languages.

NEO Personality Inventory-Revised (NEO-PI-R)

Both the MMPI-2 and the MCMI-III emphasize the abnormal or pathological aspects of the clients' personality. Both yield clinical scales that essentially indicate the extent to which a client's problems match with psychiatric diagnoses. In contrast, the NEO-PI-R is designed to measure normal personality characteristics. Specifically, the NEO-PI-R measures the five characteristics identified by decades of factor-analytic research as the fundamental traits constituting the normal personality. These five traits are (1) neuroticism, the tendency toward emotional distress, anxiety, depression; (2) extraversion, sociability or outgoingness; (3) openness, receptiveness to novel, unconventional ideas; (4) agreeableness, sympathy, cooperativeness, avoidance of interpersonal conflict; and (5) conscientiousness, organization, purposefulness, tendency to plan. Each of these five is considered a dimensional rather than categorical variable, such that a client can be rated anywhere on a spectrum from extremely high to extremely low on each. In addition to measuring each of these five traits, the NEO-PI-R also measures six "facets," or more narrowly defined components, of each of them.

The NEO-PI-R, which was published in 1992, is a 240-item, self-report, pencil-and-paper questionnaire. Each item is a single-sentence statement that the client reads and considers how it applies to him or her. Rather than true/false options, it provides clients with a 5-point scale after each item that ranges from "strongly agree" to "strongly disagree." A separate, shorter form of the test, the NEO-Five Factor Inventory (NEO-FFI), contains only 60 items but provides information only on the five personality traits, not the six facets within each. Although the reliability and validity of the NEO-PI-R have been supported by significant empirical data, the test has been criticized for lacking any measure of test-taking attitude (Costa & McCrae, 1992; Costa & Widiger, 2001). The NEO-PI-R Spanish edition includes a translated version of the test items as well as a translated version of the "Your NEO Summary Sheets" on which results can be summarized for client feedback.

California Psychological Inventory-Third Edition (CPI-III)

Whereas the NEO-PI-R deemphasizes pathology in favor of normal personality characteristics, the CPI-III steers even farther away from pathology by emphasizing positive aspects of personality. The names of its scales, including independence, self-acceptance, empathy, tolerance, responsibility, and flexibility, denote how the CPI-III highlights strengths, assets, and resources of clients rather than their psychological problems. Like the other tests described in this section, the CPI-III is a pencil-and-paper, self-report questionnaire. It includes 434 true/false items and was published in 1996. It is considered to be consistent with the positive psychology movement within the mental health field (Donnay & Elliott, 2003; Seligman & Csikszentmihalyi, 2000).

Projective Personality Tests

The assumption behind the use of projective personality tests is that clients will "project" their personalities onto ambiguous, unstructured stimuli. In other words, when people perceive and try to make sense of indefinite items, their attempts to do so reveal something about their personalities. For this reason, the essential feature of projective personality tests is the use of stimuli, most often visual, that can be perceived in a variety of ways by a variety of people. Typically, the client's task in projective personality tests is to describe what they see or how they make sense of the stimuli placed before them. They are not restricted in their responses; in other words, they can say anything that comes to mind, rather than choosing between predetermined options such as true/false or multiple choices. Scoring, interpretation, and administration of projective personality tests are often less standardized than they are for objective personality tests. Thus, the conclusions drawn by assessors from projective personality tests tend to be more inferential. These are among the strongest criticisms directed at projective personality tests, and the reasons that, especially in recent decades, some have argued against their use (e.g., Lilienfeld, Wood, & Garb, 2000). Others have responded in defense of projective personality tests (e.g., Meyer, 2004). For now, projective personality tests continue to play a significant role in psychological assessment.

Before we consider particular tests in this category, it is important to note that in recent years, the term *projective* has been replaced in some circles by the term *performance based* or *implicit*. The use of the term *performance based* emphasizes the mental tasks thought to be elicited by tests of this type, such as decision making, categorization, and "implicit dynamics and underlying templates of perception and motivation" (Meyer et al., 1998, p. 16). The use of the term *implicit* emphasizes that tests of this type, relative to objective self-report personality tests, assess aspects of personality outside awareness and are therefore more difficult to purposefully manipulate. Here, we'll use the more traditional term *projective*, but the future of tests of this type may bring more changes in nomenclature.

Rorschach Inkblot Method

The Rorschach Inkblot Method, created by Hermann Rorschach in 1921, includes 10 symmetrical inkblots, each on a separate card. Five feature only black ink, while the other five include ink of multiple colors. The blots are intended not to represent or resemble any particular object; thus, different clients may have different perceptions when viewing them. Assessors administer the Rorschach in two distinct phases. In the first phase, known as the "response" or "free association" phase, the assessor presents each inkblot to the client and asks what they might see in the card. The assessor writes down each client response verbatim. After responses to the last card are collected, the assessor begins the "inquiry" phase, in which the assessor reads the client's responses back to the client and asks the client to elaborate on them, specifying their location and the features of the blot that prompted the client to make those particular responses (Weiner, 2004).

The most popular means for scoring the Rorschach was developed by John Exner and is known as the Comprehensive System (Exner, 1986). When Hermann Rorschach created his inkblots, he created no scoring system to accompany them. So as the technique increased in popularity in the first half of the 1900s, numerous distinct scoring systems emerged. Exner's system ultimately synthesized and replaced these competing systems, such that it is highly unusual for contemporary assessors to use any other scoring system (Rose, Kaser-Boyd, & Maloney, 2001). Exner's scoring system includes normative data collected from both children and adults, so the test is appropriate for use in both of these populations. According to this system of scoring the Rorschach, each response is coded in a wide variety of ways. Among the many variables examined by the Comprehensive System are the following:

Location: the portion of the card from which the response stems, which can be as large as the whole blot or a very small detail.

Determinants: the aspects of the blot, such as its form, color, or shading, that contributed to the response.

Form quality: the extent to which the response conforms to the form of the blot, as opposed to distorting it.

Popular: the extent to which client's responses match those most frequently offered by others.

Content: the type of objects included in client responses such as people, animals, nature, food, or other categories.

Although it may seem that the content of responses—*what* clients see in the blots—might be a primary focus, interpretation of the Rorschach actually deemphasizes the importance of content. Instead, interpretation of the Rorschach emphasizes *how* clients make sense of the blots or their processing tendencies in perceiving and forming responses. This is consistent with Hermann Rorschach's original intent in creating his inkblot technique, as well as most of the variables featured in Exner's scoring system (Rose et al., 2001).

After responses are coded, numerical indices are calculated to aid in interpretation. Generally, it is presumed that the way the client makes sense of the inkblots mirrors the way the client makes sense of the world around him or her, which essentially indicates the client's personality. So clients who distort the inkblots may be likely to distort reality, clients who see very few popular responses among the blots may be unlikely to see the world conventionally, and clients whose responses consistently focus on minor details in the blot rather than larger portions or the whole blot may tend to fail to see the forest for the trees in daily life.

As stated above, the empirical standing of the Rorschach is a subject of significant controversy, with strong arguments in favor (e.g., Meyer, 2004; Rose et al., 2001) and against (e.g., Wood, Nezworski, Lilienfeld, & Garb, 2003) its reliability and validity. Among adherents of the projective method of assessing personality, the Rorschach remains very widely accepted and used.

Thematic Apperception Test (TAT)

The TAT, which was developed in the 1930s, is similar in format to the Rorschach; it involves presenting a series of cards to the client, on each of which appears an ambiguous stimulus. The primary difference between the TAT and the Rorschach is that the TAT cards present interpersonal scenes rather than inkblots. In other words, while the Rorschach inkblots could be perceived as almost anything, the TAT cards are obviously depictions of people in various situations. Clients are asked to tell a story to correspond to each card they see, considering not only the scene on the card but also what may have led to it, what may happen next, and what the people in the scene may be thinking or feeling. As the client creates stories, the assessor writes them down and may ask questions during the process to facilitate it (Bellak, 1993).

The TAT includes 31 cards altogether, but the assessor chooses only some of them, usually less than a dozen, to administer to a particular client. The process by which certain cards are chosen and others are left out is not standardized or systematic, but depends largely on the judgment of the assessor. Similarly, scoring of the TAT is typically not standardized or objective. One of its creators, Henry Murray, created a scoring technique that emphasized "needs" of the characters in the stories and "press" from the environment, but this scoring system is not often used, resulting in informal, idiosyncratic scoring that resembles art more than science (Moretti & Rossini, 2004). For these reasons, the TAT is generally not held in high regard among assessors who value tests with proven reliability and validity.

It should be noted that although the TAT can be administered to adults and children age 10 and above, variants of the TAT designed for specific age groups, including the Children's Apperception Test (CAT) and the Senior Apperception Test (SAT), are also available to assessors seeking to use projective storytelling techniques (Bellak, 1993). Projective storytelling techniques featuring more culturally diverse stimuli have also been developed. For example, the Roberts Apperception Test for Children-Second Edition offers three separate versions of its test pictures, portraying either white, black, or Hispanic individuals.

Rotter Incomplete Sentences Blank (RISB)

The RISB is the most popular sentence completion test, in which the client's task is to finish a series of unfinished sentences presented to the client on paper. So unlike the visual, nonverbal stimuli of Rorschach and TAT, the stimuli in the RISB are written sentence stems. The original RISB was published in 1950, and the most recent revisions, including separate forms for clients in high school, college, and adulthood, were published in 1992. The RISB includes 40 sentence stems on a single sheet of paper. On receiving the form, the client fills in the blank space following each sentence stem, and the presumption is that the patterns apparent from the ways the client completes the sentences are indicative of underlying personality variables. Sentence stems that resemble those appearing in the RISB include "I prefer . . .", "When I am older . . .", and "It is exciting . . ."

A formal scoring system exists for the RISB, but some assessors choose not to use it, and clinical judgment typically plays a significant role in scoring. Thus, like that of the TAT, its scientific standing is questioned by those who insist on tests with established reliability and validity. As such, the RISB is often used to complement other personality measures and to provide more personal details about the psychological problems of a particular client (Sherry, Dahlen, & Holaday, 2004).

Kinetic Family Drawing (KFD)

The KFD is one of many projective drawing techniques. Others include the draw-a-person test and the house-tree-person technique. In general, they are used more often with children than adults. They are relatively unstructured techniques in which assessors provide pencil and blank paper to clients and ask them to draw people, objects, or situations. The drawings are later analyzed by the assessor, with the assumption that various aspects of the drawings can reveal personality or developmental information about the client. That is, the assessor seeks to determine what qualities about himself or herself the client has "projected" into the drawings he or she has produced.

In the KFD, the assessor asks the children to draw a picture of their family, including themselves, doing something. The assessor may ask the client questions about the drawing to better comprehend or appreciate its content. During interpretation, the assessor may extrapolate meaning from variables such as who was included or excluded; the physical size, placement, or distance between family members; the activity in which the family is engaged, and each member's role in that activity; the extent to which the drawing is realistic; clothing, body language, and facial expressions of family members; and the like. As with many projective techniques, the scoring and interpretation of the KFD and other projective drawing techniques is subjective and idiosyncratic, especially in comparison with objective personality tests. Therefore, assessors with an empirical leaning tend not to rely on them. When they are used, they are often the first test administered in the battery, since they can serve as a relatively simple and easy "ice-breaker" for children who may be apprehensive about the assessment process.

Factors to Consider in Selecting Tests

As with tests of intelligence, achievement, and neuropsychological functioning discussed in the previous chapter, the selection of personality tests depends on the referral question and the client involved in the assessment. In this section, we seek to look beyond the obvious clinical and ethical issues involved in test selection and examine some of the other "real-world" factors involved in selecting personality tests.

The Referral Question

Some referral questions call for personality testing in the most general way, requesting a broad overview of a client's personality, or suggestions for a diagnosis without any particular hypotheses from the referral source. Others ask much more specific questions about personality, including "rule-outs" of particular disorders, or evidence of problems in a specific area of functioning. It is the assessor's responsibility to attend to the details of the referral question, and possibly to clarify or seek more information about it, before selecting personality measures to be used with a particular client. For example, consider a parent going through a divorce who is referred for personality testing as part of the custody proceedings. The referral source—the court, for example—may want a comprehensive assessment of the parent's personality to shed light on the parent's fitness to care for the children. A broad-based measure such as the MMPI-2, with its many clinical, supplementary, and content scales, might be an ideal choice for this assessment. In fact, the MMPI-2 has been used frequently in forensic cases of various kinds (Lally, 2003). On the other hand, consider a psychotherapist who has seen a client for several visits and, despite having conducted a clinical interview, is having difficulty narrowing down the client's pathology. The client's description of his problems, the psychotherapist's own relationship with the client, and the long-standing rather than episodic nature of the client's problems suggest that perhaps personality variables play a significant role. When this psychotherapist refers the client for an assessment, the psychotherapist is specifically interested in the determination of a personality disorder diagnosis. In this case, a test that emphasizes personality disorders, such as the MCMI-III, might be the best fit. Of course, there are many psychological tests that focus more narrowly than the MCMI-III on particular aspects of behavioral or emotional functioning, such as the Beck Depression Inventory-II. This test and others like it are covered in the next chapter.

In some cases, the referral question may suggest that the referral source is less interested in pathology than in strengths or normal qualities within the client. In such cases, a pathology-based instrument such as the MMPI-2 or the MCMI-III will not provide the information sought, as they essentially report the extent to which clients are pathological in a variety of categories. Instead, the NEO-PI-R, which emphasizes normal personality traits such as extroversion or agreeableness, or the CPI-III, which emphasizes personality strengths such as independence and self-acceptance, would be more appropriate choices. Of course, these tests don't lend themselves to *DSM-IV* diagnosis, but if the referral question doesn't concern diagnostic issues at all, they can be wise choices.

The referral question or additional information obtained from the referral source can also shed light on the client's motivation regarding the assessment, which can in turn influence test selection. Many clients are appropriately motivated to complete the assessment in a straightforward, forthright way. However, some may be motivated to fake good or fake bad to achieve a desired outcome, and others may be unmotivated entirely. For example, consider an adolescent referred for a full psychological evaluation by the court system after being arrested for truancy and shoplifting. The referral source shares with the assessor that the adolescent has been generally defiant and noncompliant with the court and with his parents in recent months. The assessor may be accurate in speculating that the client will be similarly noncompliant with the assessment process. The client may respond randomly to the MMPI-A, for example, or if he does pay attention to it, he may fake good to minimize negative consequences. So if the assessor uses the MMPI-A, its validity scales should be emphasized. Some assessors may choose to rely on projective tests in a situation of this type, because they are more difficult to fake, and they require more effort to reject due to their interpersonal rather than pencil-and-paper format.

The Client's Culture and Language

Cultural competence should always be a top priority, and for an assessor, test selection is an important component of cultural competence. To begin, the assessor should be careful to select tests that are appropriate for the client's linguistic abilities and preferences. This is especially true for personality assessment, in which many of the common instruments require extensive reading. The most popular of these instruments, including the MMPI tests, are available in multiple languages. Even if a client is administered a pencil-and-paper personality test in his or her preferred language, there may be particular words or phrases that are confusing or easily misunderstood by members of particular cultural groups. If suspected, this can be explored by the assessor with the client and commented on in the report.

Beyond language in its written form, assessors should be sensitive to issues of spoken language as well. The projective tests, for example, rely heavily on the client's understanding of the assessor's spoken instructions, and the assessor's ability to transcribe the client's spoken words into written responses. Especially during the process of writing down client responses, assessors should remember that a client's statements should be appreciated in the context of their own culture, and that the assessor runs the risk of misunderstanding or overpathologizing the client if the assessor imposes his or her own meaning on a client's words. For example, imagine a client responding to a TAT card that depicts an elderly person. Various ethnicities hold very different beliefs toward the elderly, including their place in the family and the extent to which they should be respected or revered. If the assessor's ethnic background is different from that of the client, the assessor should be careful to assign meaning to the client's comments about the elderly person within the context of the client's—not the assessor's—culture.

The Client's Age

Often, client age leads directly to the choice of certain personality tests over others. If a client is 15 years old, the MMPI-A is more appropriate than the MMPI-2, but if the client is 51 years old, the MMPI-2 is the obvious choice. However, there are some cases in which complications arise in personality test selection related to the age of the client. For example, the age of 18 is the borderline between the MMPI-A and the MMPI-2. Both tests include norms for 18-year-olds, so the assessor must give thought to the choice of test for clients of this age. The MMPI-A manual recommends decisions on a "case-by-base" basis and goes on to offer only one "suggested guideline"—that the MMPI-A should be administered to 18-year-olds in high school, while the MMPI-2 should be administered to 18-year-olds in college, working, or otherwise living independently (Butcher et al., 1992, p. 23). For younger clients, there is some judgment involved in the lower age limit of the MMPI-A. Its norms go as low as age 14, but its manual says that "it is possible that bright, mature, younger (12- or 13-year-old) adolescents can comprehend and respond validly to the MMPI-A" (p. 23). Regardless of the test selected, personality tests administered to individuals at or near the age boundaries should be interpreted cautiously.

Time Restrictions

When referral questions have no deadline attached, assessors have the luxury of selecting tests with no consideration of how long they might take. In the real world, however, personality assessment must take place within a particular time frame. In such cases, a careful selection of tests can be important. The MMPI-2 and the MMPI-A, despite their popularity and strong reliability and validity, can be time-consuming tests. This is particularly true for certain clients, including those who read slowly or those with obsessive-compulsive tendencies who may reread questions many times or fret over how they have marked the answer sheet. The manuals of the MMPI-A and the MMPI-2 both describe abbreviated versions of the test, with the first 350 and 370 items, respectively, providing enough data to calculate the basic clinical scales, but these abbreviated versions can't provide as much information as the full versions (Butcher, Dahlstrom, Graham, Tellegen, & Kaemmer, 1989; Butcher et al., 1992). Other objective tests can provide more time-efficient alternatives to the MMPI-2 and the MMPI-A, including the MCMI-III, the NEO-PI-R, and especially the NEO-FFI.

The notion of multimethod assessment deserves mention in our discussion of time restrictions in personality assessment. Multimethod assessment refers to the practice of using multiple tests rather than relying on one, with the knowledge that no single test is perfect, and results merit confidence to the extent that multiple measures converge on them. For these reasons, assessors should never cut corners by eliminating necessary tests, even if they overlap with others. Of course, multimethod assessment can reach a point of overkill, and assessors shouldn't administer tests unnecessarily, but time pressure doesn't justify dropping essential tests either. In some cases, a referral question simply can't be adequately addressed in the time allotted. In these situations, the assessor is wise to request more time or politely explain that the proper assessment can't be conducted.

What to Include in the Assessment Report and How to Include It

How much background information should I include about each test? It may be helpful to include a brief statement about each test as it is introduced. Although assessors and other mental health professionals may associate the name or acronym of a test with its purpose or domain, it cannot be assumed that other readers will. For example, when the MMPI-2 results are reported, it can be beneficial to include a statement along the lines of

> The MMPI-2 is a broad-based measure of personality that provides information on the extent to which an adult client endorses a variety of psychological problems. It is a pencil-and-paper tests in which the client reads sentences and responds "true" or "false" regarding whether the statement applies to himself or herself.

Or, when reporting Rorschach results, it can be helpful to include a statement such as

> The Rorschach is a personality test in which the client is presented with ambiguous inkblots and asked to tell what he or she sees in them. The pattern of responses provided by the client are thought to reveal underlying personality characteristics.

Brief descriptions such as these can familiarize the reader with the purpose and method of the tests, thereby enhancing their understanding of the report.

Of course, the assessor should keep in mind that educating the reader about various tests is not the primary purpose of the report. Background information about reports should therefore be kept to a minimum. Readers can always seek clarification from the assessor or from other sources.

How should I organize the results of a particular test? The most comprehensible way to present results of a test is typically to offer the primary findings first, followed by the less remarkable findings. This can be a bit more challenging with personality tests than with intelligence or achievement tests, since the hierarchical structure of intelligence and achievement tests lends itself to the reporting of results in order of decreasing scale; that is, full-scale IQ score, followed by index or factor IQ scores, and then by subtest scores. For many personality tests, the most clinically notable findings merit first mention. For example, if an MMPI-2 profile includes an elevation of two clinical scales, an interpretation of the corresponding two-scale code would be an appropriate place to begin discussing the MMPI-2 results. Elevations in supplementary or content scales would be secondary. Of course, if a single pattern permeates all these areas, describing that pattern can be an appropriate lead, or if the validity scales are most important—particularly if they invalidate the test—they can be given first mention. Other personality tests, such as the NEO-PI-R, offer a structure that is somewhat hierarchical. In this case, it would be wise to discuss the client's scores on the five factors of personality before delving into an analysis of the client's scores on the six facet scores that fall under each of these factors.

Should my report include specific test scores as opposed to summaries? When assessors write the results of an IQ or achievement test, they often include the "numbers" themselves—full-scale scores, factor/index scores, subtest scores, and so on. Including "numbers" with the results of personality tests is less common. It is more typical for assessment reports to include only verbal summaries of the results of personality tests than to include specific numbers, such as a client's score on a validity or clinical scale of the MMPI-2, or a client's Form Quality Index on the Rorschach. Regardless of the reasons for this discrepancy, assessors should think carefully about including specific scores from personality tests in their reports. Most important, will inclusion of such numbers enhance or hinder the reader's understanding of the results? If the reader is a fellow mental health professional with expertise in the personality test in question, the inclusion of a table of MMPI-2 or MCMI-III scores may be helpful. However, if the reader lacks the training to make sense of the numbers, their inclusion could be confusing or might obscure the verbal interpretations that also appear in the report. This is especially true with personality tests in which the "whole" does not necessarily equal the "sum of the parts." For example, consider a client whose MMPI-A profile yields elevated scores on clinical scales 2 (depression), 4 (psychopathic deviate), and 8 (schizophrenia). It would be misguided to consider these three elevated scores each in isolation; instead, they should be interpreted as a three-scale code type. Descriptions of a 2/4/8 code type on the MMPI-A do not simply list depressive, antisocial, and schizophrenic characteristics; instead, their combination produces a complex, nuanced clinical profile that represents something other than a rote compilation of the three elevated scales. Depending on the reader, the inclusion of a table of MMPI-A clinical scale scores for this client might mistakenly suggest that each scale can stand alone in terms of interpretation, when it is actually more clinically responsible to consider them in conjunction with each other, as would appear in the verbal summary of the results.

To what extent should my report incorporate behavioral observations? Observations of client behavior during the process of personality testing can be essential to include in the assessment report. In some cases, such observations can be as informative as the test results themselves. For example, consider a client taking the TAT. When the assessor presents the first card, the client studies it intently for a full 3 minutes before beginning to tell a story corresponding to it. After a few words of the story, the client stops, pauses, and starts again from the beginning, attempting to tell the story "perfectly" from beginning to end. This time, the client gets a few sentences in, pauses, and again restarts from the beginning. In all, the client restarted the story six times before he could state it without any "mistakes." The client displayed a similar pattern on all the cards, which caused the TAT to take an inordinately long time to complete. Regardless of whether the content of the client's stories included references to obsessive-compulsive behavior, the client's behavior during the process of telling the stories certainly suggests obsessive-compulsive tendencies. As another example, consider a client who takes an objective personality questionnaire such as the MMPI-2 and worriedly asks dozens of questions about the precise meaning of its items. A reasonable number of questions are unremarkable, but excessive questioning, particularly when fueled by worry, can be indicative of underlying anxiety issues. The assessor's observation of these anxious tendencies deserves mention in the report regardless of results yielded by the tests.

CHAPTER 6

Gathering Information

Clinical Interviews, Review of Records, and Measures of Behavioral and Emotional Functioning

This chapter focuses on the wide variety of clinical interviews used by assessors, as well as a sampling of some specific approaches used to assess behavioral and emotional functioning. These approaches include symptom and behavior checklists, both broad-based and more specialized varieties, behavioral assessment, and reviewing records. As in the previous two chapters, our intent is to review basic information about each method of assessment and to discuss "real-world" issues that arise regarding their use.

Clinical Interviews

Clinical interviews vary widely because they serve an array of different purposes. In clinical practice, there are a number of approaches to interviews, but for the sake of simplicity, most can be described as belonging to one of the following categories:

- *Intake interviews*, in which the purpose is to gain an understanding of the current issues to determine whether to "intake" the client to the agency for treatment.

- *Diagnostic interviews*, in which the purpose is to determine and assign the appropriate diagnosis or diagnoses to the client.

- *Mental status examinations*, typically conducted in medical settings or with clients with serious mental illness or dementia, in which the purpose is to briefly and accurately provide a description of a client's current level of functioning across a range of domains.

- *Crisis interviews*, in which the purpose is to assess and offer immediate intervention, either in person or on the phone, for clients whose situations require urgent attention. Examples of such situations include a client who is suicidal or who otherwise is a threat to harm himself or herself or another person.

- *Assessment interviews* (Groth-Marnat, 1999) or clinical assessment interviews, in which the purpose is to gather relevant information to use in the psychological assessment. Assessment interviews sometimes incorporate a mental status exam or diagnostic interview, and on rare occasions, they become crisis interviews. Assessments of children usually include an interview with parents or guardians, and assessments of children and adults sometimes include interviews with collateral informants.

A key question for contemporary clinicians is the extent to which the clinical interview will be structured versus unstructured. In a structured interview, the questions are preplanned, and the interviewer follows them in a particular sequence. In other words, the questions that the interviewer asks are scripted ahead of time. Published structured interviews, most of which focus on formal diagnosis, have proliferated in recent years, and include the Structured Clinical Interview for *DSM-IV* Disorders (First, Spitzer, Gibbon, & Williams, 1997b), the Brown ADD Diagnostic Forms (Brown, 2005), the Anxiety Disorders Interview Schedule-Revised (Di Nardo & Barlow, 1988), and the Asperger Syndrome Diagnostic Interview (Gillberg, Gillberg, Rastam, & Wentz, 2001), among others. In contrast, in an unstructured interview, there is no such preplanning or scripting. Instead, interviewers extemporize creatively, deciding what to ask as the interview takes place. Of course, there is a middle ground between structured and unstructured interviews—semistructured interviews— balancing some degree of predetermined questioning and on-the-spot improvising.

Structured interviews offer particular advantages and disadvantages. Structured interviews tend to be empirically well regarded, especially because of their high reliability across interviewers, they are standardized and uncomplicated, and they minimize clinical judgment while maximizing objectivity. On the other hand, they have a rigid format, which can impede rapport and the client's explanations, and many are overly thorough, resulting in an interview that takes too long to conduct. Unstructured interviews have strengths and weaknesses as well—they can be customized for a client's particular issues, allow for client elaborations, and can facilitate rapport; however, they tend to demonstrate low reliability, they are not standardized, and they depend heavily on clinical judgment.

Semistructured interviews offer some features of both structured and unstructured interviews. For most situations in which assessment is being conducted for clinical (as opposed to research) purposes, semistructured interviews strike an ideal balance. The unstructured interview is too free flowing and not conducive to obtaining answers to all the questions the assessment clinician needs answered. The structured interview does not provide information that is clinically relevant but outside the boundaries of predetermined questions. The semistructured interview can be as long or as short as the clinician has time for and the client can tolerate. It can cover a lot of ground or a little, and it can explore all kinds of areas that are important to sort out. There is a lot of room for the clinician's personal style to come through, with no one correct approach to eliciting the cooperation of the client, and for many clinicians it is both challenging and satisfying work. In addition, while the client is answering questions, the clinician has the opportunity to observe her thought processes, mood, affect, judgment, insight, hygiene, grooming, eye contact, and numerous other relevant factors. However, on the negative side, there is no manual that describes how to build rapport, and there are no directions to tell the clinician what to ask or how to judge the accuracy of the information he obtains. We offer the following guidelines for conducting effective semistructured assessment interviews. (Note that the guidelines apply to most, but not all, assessment situations. Supervision prior to the assessment interview is essential, especially in dealing with challenging situations, such as assessing inmates in a correctional facility, assessing clients who have a reason to be deceptive or manipulative, or those who are psychotic or extremely anxious or depressed.)

1. Introduce the interview in a language the client can readily understand by describing its purpose, what will be done with the information, and limits to confidentiality. Obtain the client's consent.

2. Be prepared with a list of questions, some that are easy and comfortable for both the client and the clinician and others that are more difficult but specifically relevant to referral questions. Easy questions build trust and rapport and help the clinician regulate the client's level of comfort and, conversely, anxiety. They allow the clinician to judge how to ask the client about certain things or, in some instances, whether to avoid asking certain questions altogether.

3. Aim for empathy and understanding. This will help you ask the right questions.

4. Maintain a nonjudgmental attitude. This will help the client feel more comfortable disclosing personal information and will help you remain calm and objective regardless of information that is shared.

5. Keep in mind that the purpose of the interview is assessment, not treatment. It is important not to confuse the two, although moving a client to accept treatment or to feel hopeful can sometimes be both necessary and appropriate.

6. Pay attention to "countertransference" reactions; that is, to your emotional responses to the client. Some of your responses may be quite personal and need to be managed so as not to interfere with professional work. Perhaps, for example, you had a bad experience with a similar client in the past and you are feeling unusually nervous. More often, however, the psychologist's emotional responses (to a client in an assessment interview) are related to the client's patterns of interpersonal interaction and can be an important clue to understanding the client's personality dynamics or other aspects of her functioning. It is important for the novice psychologist to know that emotional responses to a client are a normal part of the assessment process and can, and often should, be discussed in supervision.

7. Make a point of not leaving anything out that is essential to the assessment, by referring to a list of necessary information (such as the medication a client takes, his grade in school, or other facts) before concluding the interview.

8. Remember that interviewing skills, like other skills, improve with practice and experience. Your first several interviews should be adequate, but they don't have to be perfect.

Interviewing Parents and Guardians

When children and teenagers are assessed, parents or guardians provide the background information needed to fully understand the child's problems and strengths and the context they occur in. Parents or guardians typically provide the developmental history as well as information about the family structure, family history, and family stresses. An interview with family members also sheds light on family dynamics, and importantly, provides information about family members' concerns about the child and their thoughts on what might be wrong and what might be helpful.

An interview with parents or guardians is simplest to conduct when the child is not present. In this situation, the family member does not have to be concerned about the impact of the information he presents on the child, or about talking about the child in her presence. An assessment of the parent-child relationship can also be conducted by interviewing the parent and child together and examining how they interact. Note that these two types of interviews provide very different kinds of information, and a comprehensive assessment may require both of them.

When interviewing parents or guardians, keep in mind that they offer their own perspectives, and these are sometimes distorted or self-serving. They also may be more or less cooperative and more or less insightful and informative. They may have their own problems, such as cognitive deficits or mental illness. Regardless, it is helpful to focus the parent interview in two areas, obtaining neutral facts and subjective opinions. The psychologist should be prepared to ask general questions that are relevant to the assessment of children in most circumstances as well as questions that are specifically relevant to the reason for referral. General questions include those about the child's early developmental history, family structure, living situation, academic progress, interests, quality of relationships with peers and family members, and parental concerns. Specific questions might be about progress in reading, writing, math, or other academic areas; concentration and activity level; treatment history; trauma history; emotional functioning; and so forth, depending on the purpose of the assessment. Asking the parent's opinion about the child's problems and how to solve them provides vital contextual information. In addition, the parent's responses to such questions have important implications for recommendations that follow from the assessment.

Interviewing Collateral Informants

Collateral informants are individuals, other than parents or guardians, who have information to share about the client who is being assessed. Teachers, therapists, social workers, attorneys, physicians, friends, and relatives can provide information relevant and sometimes indispensable to the assessment. Interviews with collateral informants are often brief and focused, and they may take place during a phone call rather than a visit. It is helpful to be prepared with specific questions for the informant and also to give her an opportunity to discuss her concerns or thoughts about the client more generally. As with parent interviews, the informant may have her own agenda and point of view, and it is important for the psychologist to separate facts from opinions, although both are relevant. Note that it is essential to obtain written permission (a signed "release of information" form) from the client to contact the collateral informant, as is true in any situation in which the client's confidentiality must be protected.

When should interviews with collateral informants be conducted? Depending on the circumstances of the assessment, information from collateral informants might be necessary to understand certain aspects of the client's situation, things that don't make sense because the client cannot or does not provide sufficient information herself. A collateral informant can also provide observations about the client's behavior in a given circumstance, such as at work, in the classroom, or in the therapist's office. Note that obtaining information from a collateral informant is different from talking over the circumstances of the referral with the person making it. It is not about why the referral was made, but about answering referral questions by gathering relevant information from the people who have access to it.

Review of Records

Reviewing client records—typically, documents that provide information about previous assessments, treatment, educational history, medical history, legal history, or other background—can be a vital component of some assessments. Experience with this practice will reveal one truth—records are unpredictable. The clinician doesn't have control over which records are made available or their comprehensiveness. The records are created for purposes other than the clinician's and, although they may seem to present "facts," such as whether the client was previously hospitalized, the facts may not be accurate. Yet they often contain crucial information that is unavailable elsewhere, and they formally document the client's educational, medical, psychiatric, or legal history.

Information in records can be used to develop questions for the interview, for example, "I saw in your records that you were expelled from school in April. Can you tell me what happened?" They can also be used directly, for example, to find out what medication a client was taking at the time of her last admission to the hospital, or how far she went in school. Finally, a record might contain information that is discrepant or unique. It may describe that the client was hearing voices, made a suicide attempt, became violent, refused treatment, or almost anything else. The clinician has to sort out what to do with the information, especially if it doesn't fit with other findings. There are two reasons for this. The most obvious is that the clinician needs to take that information into account in developing his conceptualization of the client and his problems and for his efforts to make useful recommendations. If the client has always refused treatment in the past, it doesn't make sense to simply recommend a new treatment program. The other reason is less obvious but also important. The readers of the report may know the information that is in the records. If the clinician ignores it, the reader may not view the report as credible.

Symptom and Behavior Checklists

Symptom and behavior checklists come in a variety of forms and lengths. They share the purpose of cataloging clients' symptoms of psychological disorders and problems, including external symptoms such as observable behaviors and internal symptoms such as thoughts and feelings. They are often self-reports, but some include versions in which someone close to the client acts as an informant by providing information about the client. Some are comprehensive, covering a broad spectrum of psychological problems, while briefer variations tend to target specific areas.

Broad-Based Symptoms and Behavior Checklists

Symptom Checklist-90-Revised (SCL-90-R)

The SCL-90-R is a symptom checklist for adult and adolescent clients age 13 and above. It covers a wide range of psychological problems and disorders. It is a self-report, pencil-and-paper questionnaire containing 90 items, each of which briefly describes a particular symptom. The client chooses a response from among five options indicating the extent to which he or she experiences each symptom. The SCL-90-R provides scores in nine separate symptom dimensions, including depression, anxiety, hostility, phobic anxiety, paranoid ideation, psychoticism, somatization, obsessive-compulsive symptoms, and interpersonal sensitivity. It also yields a Global Severity Index that suggests an overall level of psychological distress for the client. For adult clients, norms are available for inpatients, outpatients, and nonpatients. A sizeable body of research supports the reliability and validity of the SCL-90-R. Typical administration takes about 15 to 20 minutes.

Child Behavior Checklist (CBCL)

The CBCL is a checklist of problem behaviors designed for children age 6 to 18. Parents or other close relatives of the child complete the form regarding the behavior of the child client. The CBCL includes 118 items, each of which briefly describes a problem behavior. Raters indicate the applicability of each statement to the child client by choosing one of three options: (1) not true, (2) somewhat or sometimes true, and (3) very or often true. The domains of behavior measured by the subscales of the CBCL span a wide range, and include aggressive behavior, anxious/depressed, attention problems, rule-breaking behavior, social problems, somatic complaints, thought problems, and withdrawn/depressed. The Teacher's Report Form and the Youth Self-Report Form for children age 11 to 18 are variations of the CBCL in which teachers or the child himself or herself respond to the items regarding the child's behavior. Assessors can use multiple questionnaires to solicit information from more than one source.

The CBCL is part of a larger family of checklists contained in the Achenbach System of Empirically Based Assessment. Also included in this system are an adaptation of the CBCL for children age 1.5 to 5, with versions for both parents/guardians and caregivers/teachers, as well as checklists appropriate for the assessment of adults (Adult Behavior Checklist and Adult Self-Report) and older adults (Older Adult Behavior Checklist and Older Adult Self-Report). Tests in the Achenbach System of Empirically Based Assessment have been translated into many languages, and some offer norms based on particular cultural groups from around the globe.

Targeted Symptom and Behavior Checklists

Relatively brief symptom checklists focusing on particular areas of functioning are available for a tremendous variety of psychological problems. Here, we focus on a sampling commonly used by psychological assessors which happen to assess depression, anxiety, attention-deficit/hyperactivity, and eating problems.

Beck Depression Inventory-II (BDI-II)

As its name indicates, the BDI-II assesses symptoms of depression in clients age 13 to 80. It is a very brief measure, containing only 21 items and requiring only about 5 minutes to administer. The BDI-II is a self-report, pencil-and-paper questionnaire with a multiple-choice format, such that the client chooses one of four statements that best describes his or her experience of a particular symptom. The BDI-II yields a total score, which reflects overall depression. It also contains a few items that can indicate suicidality, but a separate test, the Beck Hopelessness Scale, assesses this issue in more detail. Psychometric data for the BDI-II are quite strong, making it a reliable, valid depression screen used frequently by assessors in many settings. In addition to its original English version, a Spanish version of the BDI-II is also available.

Beck Anxiety Inventory (BAI)

Also authored by Aaron Beck, the BAI is quite similar to the BDI-II in format, but its focus is anxiety rather than depression. It is appropriate for clients age 17 to 80. Like the BDI-II, the BAI contains just 21 items and can be completed in 5 to 10 minutes. It is a self-report, pencil-and-paper questionnaire in which clients choose one of four options to describe the level of each particular symptom of anxiety. Both psychological and somatic symptoms of anxiety are included, as are symptoms of specific anxiety disorders such as panic disorder, obsessive-compulsive disorder, and generalized anxiety disorder. Like the BDI-II, the BAI is available in Spanish as well as English.

Conners' Rating Scales-Revised (CRS-R)

The CRS-R assesses symptoms of attention-deficit/hyperactivity disorder (ADHD) in children age 3 to 17. Although it can provide information on other psychological problems, especially those frequently comorbid with ADHD, the assessment of ADHD itself is its focal point. It is a pencil-and-paper questionnaire that can be completed by the child's parent/guardian, teacher, or the child himself or herself if the child is 12 to 17 years old. Each of these variations has both a long and short form, with the long forms containing 59 to 87 items and the short forms containing 27 to 28 items. Assessors can choose to use more than one version of the test to gather information about the child's behavior from multiple sources. The CRS-R is available in Spanish as well as English.

Eating Disorder Inventory-3 (EDI-3)

The EDI-3 measures symptoms and constructs related to eating disorders. It is a self-report, pencil-and-paper questionnaire appropriate for clients age 13 to 53. It includes 91 items, and typically takes about 20 minutes to complete. It yields scores on 12 scales, 3 of which are specific to eating disorders and 9 of which are relevant but not central to eating disorders. The manual of the EDI-3 provides normative data for clients with specific eating disorders, such as anorexia—restricting type, anorexia—binge-eating/purging type, and bulimia. A separate questionnaire, the EDI-3 Symptom Checklist, is a brief screen more directly tied to *DSM-IV* criteria for eating disorders but providing fewer details than the full EDI-3.

Vineland Adaptive Behavior Scales-Second Edition (Vineland-II)

The Vineland-II measures personal and social skills needed for self-sufficient everyday living, and as such, is a popular tool in determining mental retardation diagnoses and other problems involving developmental disabilities. It assesses the domains of communication, daily living skills, socialization, motor skills, and maladaptive behavior, with two to three subtests covering each of these areas. The Vineland-II offers a variety of formats, including a Parent/Caregiver Rating Form and a Teacher Rating Form, each of which requires the rater to respond regarding the client's behavior when under his or her supervision. Semistructured interviews of parents or caregivers are also available. An adaptation of the Vineland-II for Spanish-speaking clients and informants is available. A revision of the Vineland targeting clients in early childhood—the Vineland Social-Emotional Early Childhood Scales (Vineland SEEC)—has also been developed.

Behavior Assessment System for Children-Second Edition (BASC-2)

The BASC-2 is intended to measure the behavior and emotions of clients from ages 2 to 21 years. It can help in the determination of psychological, behavioral, or educational problems that are often noted in individualized education programs (IEPs), and the information it yields can lead to effective interventions by therapists or school personnel. The BASC-2 incorporates information from three perspectives—client, teacher, and parent. Rating scales are offered for all three to complete (assuming the child is age 8 or above), and additional techniques are available for parents and teachers. Like the Vineland-II, the BASC-2 yields some scores on adaptive scales: activities of daily living, adaptability, functional communication, leadership, social skills, and study skills. In addition, the BASC-2 also yields some scores on clinical scales: aggression, anxiety, attention problems, atypicality, conduct problems, depression, hyperactivity, learning problems, somatization, and withdrawal. BASC-2 forms are available in Spanish as well as English.

Behavioral Assessment

The assessment techniques discussed thus far involve asking clients, or others who know the client well, to describe their behavior via responses to questionnaires. An assumption implicit in the use of these assessment techniques is that the behaviors in question are signs of underlying problems. In other words, from the behaviors, the assessor can infer the presence of a psychological disorder. An alternative approach to assessment—behavioral assessment—rejects these assumptions. Behavioral assessors believe that the problem behaviors are not signs of underlying issues but are samples of the problem itself. That is, problem behaviors should not be viewed as symptoms; instead, they should be addressed directly. Moreover, behavioral assessors argue that inference decreases the quality of assessment. Thus, to the extent possible, the assessor should assess behavior directly rather than indirectly, eliminating the need to infer conclusions from the data collected. Such direct assessment most often takes the form of behavioral observation, which is also known as naturalistic observation. So if an assessor receives a referral about a child who is disruptive in her classroom, a behavioral assessment approach would involve the assessor visiting the child's classroom to observe and systematically record the child's behavior rather than asking the teacher, parent, or child herself to complete questionnaires about her behavior. Firsthand assessment of this type does not rely on the reports of the client or others about the client's behavior, which can be intentionally or unintentionally inaccurate. When behavioral observation takes place, target behaviors are clearly defined, and the frequency, duration, or intensity of the behavior is measured over predetermined periods of time. Often, the antecedents and consequences of the target behavior are tracked as well (Ollendick, Alvarez, & Greene, 2004).

Factors to Consider in Selecting Assessment Methods

Each client or referral question calls for a unique consideration of options regarding interviews, symptom checklists, and behavioral assessment. Of course, reliability and validity should be top priorities in the selection of specific assessment methods within these categories. Here, we consider some additional, real-world issues that can influence the selection of assessment methods.

The Referral Question

The degree of specificity of the referral question can determine the appropriateness of certain symptom and behavior checklists and the type of interview that would be most helpful. In some cases, the referral source may know very little about the client, or may want the assessor to "cast a wide net" to identify any psychological problems the client may have. In such cases, a broad-based checklist such as the SCL-90-R for adults or the CBCL for children, along with a semistructured interview, is a good choice. In other cases, the referral source is quite familiar with the client or has suspicions that problems of a certain type may be present. In these cases, the referral question may mention specific areas such as depression, anxiety, ADHD, or eating disorders, and a correspondingly specific checklist and, in some instances, a structured diagnostic interview, would be appropriate. Of course, assessors can use broad and specific measures consecutively in an attempt to identify problem areas and subsequently gather more detailed knowledge about them.

The Client's Culture and Language

During interviews, client behavior should always be appreciated within a cultural context. Both what a client says and how he or she interacts with the interviewer can be strongly influenced by cultural factors. The assessor must be careful not to impose his or her own meaning onto the actions or words of clients from diverse cultures, as doing so could result in misinterpretation or overpathologizing. When cultures differ between assessor and client, it is advisable to openly acknowledge and discuss these differences rather than ignoring them. Doing so can enhance both rapport and understanding (Sommers-Flanagan & Sommers-Flanagan, 1999).

Of course, appreciation of a client's culture does not equate to knowing the norms or tendencies within that culture and expecting the client to epitomize them. In other words, there is tremendous variability among individuals within a culture, so assessors should be aware of what is "typical" within a culture while at the same time realizing that any particular client might be culturally "atypical." Having said this, specific patterns of interpersonal communication have been identified as common within particular ethnic groups. For example, compared with whites, Asian Americans tend to speak relatively softly and avoid eye contact, especially with perceived authority figures, such as psychologists, and Native Americans tend to speak relatively slowly and exhibit an indirect gaze (e.g., Sue & Sue, 2003). Culture can be defined by variables other than ethnicity, some of which can be very relevant to the interaction within the clinical interview. For example, men and women exhibit different norms of verbal communication, such that men use speech in a more goal-oriented, assertive manner, while women use speech more to build relationships and to self-disclose (Mio, Barker-Hackett, & Tumambing, 2006; Wood, 1994, 1999). The selection of interviews, and of particular techniques within an interview, should be made with awareness of these cultural issues.

The Client's Motivation

Some clients are motivated to complete the assessment, and to do so straightforwardly and honestly. Others may be entirely unmotivated or may be motivated to present themselves falsely. For appropriately motivated clients, symptom and behavior checklists can provide an accurate description of their problems across broad areas or more specific domains. However, for those inclined to present themselves untrustworthily, behavioral assessment can be a wise choice. Consider, for example, a 13-year-old boy referred for hyperactivity in the classroom. On symptom checklists such as the CBCL or the CRS-R, all parties may be motivated to either exaggerate or minimize symptoms. The child's teachers may exaggerate symptoms with the intention of increasing the odds that the child will be diagnosed and subsequently medicated, thereby reducing classroom disruptions or facilitating removal from their classes; one parent may be motivated to exaggerate to secure an ADHD diagnosis so their health insurance company will pay for treatment; another parent may be motivated to minimize in hopes of maintaining the belief that his or her child isn't "abnormal"; and the child himself or herself may be motivated to exaggerate or minimize for any of the above reasons or a host of others. Direct behavioral observation sidesteps all these potential biases by allowing the assessor to view the problem firsthand.

Similarly, the motivation of the client can influence the assessor's choices regarding the interview. For example, although the referral question may require the assessor to conduct a diagnostic interview or a mental status exam, conclusions drawn from either can be influenced by a client's tendency to exaggerate or minimize symptoms during the interview. Also, for clients who lack motivation and volunteer little during an interview of any kind, the assessor may choose to seek information from others who know the client well, with the client's permission when required. Such sources can also provide valuable data when the client is resistant to completing symptom or behavior checklists, particularly when the checklist is available in versions other than self-report, such as the CBCL and the CRS-R.

The Likelihood of the Assessor Conducting Therapy With the Client

In many situations, the assessor will assess the client and never see him or her again. In others, the assessor is likely to become the client's therapist. Foresight about this distinction can guide the selection of particular interview types by an assessor. For example, consider the use of the Structured Clinical Interview for *DSM-IV* Disorders (SCID; First, Gibbon, Spitzer, Williams, & Benjamin, 1997; First, Spitzer, Gibbon, & Williams, 1997a, 1997b). The SCID is a specific protocol, a list of questions designed around criteria for many of the disorders in the *DSM-IV*. As such, it has all the benefits of structured interviews more generally, including demonstrable reliability and validity, as well as the ability to definitively yield answers to questions of diagnosis. On the other hand, structured interviews such as the SCID have a rather rigid format, forcing assessors to ask preplanned yes/no questions and clients to correspondingly provide brief, unelaborated answers. With some clients, this can hinder the establishment of rapport and interfere with the formation of a therapeutic relationship. If the assessor cares more about accurately diagnosing the client and less about establishing rapport that can be carried over into a therapy relationship, a structured diagnostic interview can be ideal. However, if the assessor knows from the beginning that the assessment client is likely to become a therapy client, a semistructured or unstructured interview—allowing for more natural give-and-take, rapport, and relationship building—may be advantageous.

Time Restrictions

When little time is available for the assessment, certain assessment methods are more feasible than others. For example, certain interviews are typically shorter than others; in fact, the mental status exam was designed with speed in mind. On the other hand, intake interviews can be somewhat lengthy, as can diagnostic interviews, especially when they are conducted with a client for whom prospective diagnostic categories have not been identified, necessitating the exploration of many categories. Repeated behavioral observations are also time-consuming. Time limitations can also hinder the number of people involved in an assessment. For example, the option of collecting data from teachers, parents, or others who know the client well via instruments such as the CRS-R or the CBCL might need to be eliminated if doing so requires phone calls to make arrangements and time delays, common in busy individuals such as teachers and parents, in completing the forms. In such cases, the assessor may need to rely more heavily on information from more accessible individuals—most notably, the client. Of course, the assessor always has the option of declining the referral or requesting more time, and should do so rather than rushing excessively or reaching conclusions without appropriate information from relevant parties.

What to Include in the Assessment Report and How to Include It

How much background information should I include about each method? As with tests of other types such as intelligence, achievement, and personality tests, a brief description of the nature and purpose of a test can help readers understand its results. This description need not be longer than a sentence or two, as the objective is merely to familiarize the readers rather than educate them in detail about the test. For example, when presenting the results of the SCL-90-R, it can be beneficial to begin with a description along the lines of "The SCL-R-90 is a written questionnaire covering a broad range of psychological problems. Clients read each item and respond by choosing one of five options to indicate the extent to which they agree." It is less common, and probably less necessary, to offer a description of the kind of clinical interview that took place, largely because the delineation between interviews is not as clear-cut as that between written instruments. However, if a particular published interview, such as the SCID was used, a brief description is in order.

How should I organize the results of a particular method? Should I integrate results across methods, or should I report each test result separately? The results of symptom and behavior checklists, structured interviews, and behavioral assessments are typically reported straightforwardly. General findings are reported first and narrower or more specific results are reported next. If the referral question highlights a particular issue, results most relevant to that issue can be mentioned first as appropriate. Findings from record reviews are sometimes included in the background section of the report and not mentioned otherwise. However, if a record review is lengthy or specifically relevant to referral questions (e.g., the documented history supports important conclusions from the current assessment), findings from the review are reported separately, prior to test results. Findings from semistructured interviews contribute to background information and are reported in that section, but they are also described separately in the report, usually prior to test results or behavioral assessment data. As with other test data, all findings are ultimately integrated in the summary or conclusions section of the report.

Regarding the interview, it is important to report results in such a way that the words of the client or other interviewee are not presented as a fact in the report; in most cases, the claims made by clients or others being interviewed can't be substantiated directly by the assessor. For example, if a client named Dennis states during an interview that his anxiety has interfered significantly with his sleep, it is better to write "Dennis reports that his anxiety has interfered significantly with his sleep," rather than "Dennis's anxiety has interfered significantly with his sleep." To avoid awkward wording in sentence after sentence, an alternative is to begin a paragraph or section of the report with a statement along the lines of "The information reported in this [paragraph/section/etc.] was provided by [Dennis/Dennis's mother/Dennis's father/etc.]." See Chapter 8 for more detailed information about organizing and reporting interview and record review data.

Should my report include specific test scores as opposed to summaries? It is somewhat unusual to include specific scores such as global/total or subscale from symptom and behavior checklists. In this regard, they are more similar to personality tests than to intelligence or achievement tests. It is more typical to include verbal descriptions of the results. For example, in reporting the results of the BDI-II, it is more common to mention that a client's total score fell in the "moderate" range of depression than to mention the total score itself. If specific numbers are listed, assessors must remember that untrained readers will need accompanying verbal descriptions to make sense of them. Including the numbers without an explanation is an irresponsible way to present results.

To what extent should my report incorporate behavioral observations? Clinical interviews yield a wealth of behavioral observations, and they should not be ignored when completing the report. Concentrating on what a client says to the exclusion of how he behaves during the interview can result in the loss of crucial information. Symptom and behavior checklists may not provide quite as much opportunity for behavioral observation, as they generally take the form of self-report, written questionnaires rather than a face-to-face interaction; however, in some instances, they can provide important information. For example, certain clients will complete the questionnaires sloppily or neatly, slowly or quickly, indifferently or assiduously, with or without complaining, with or without bizarre comments, and so on. Any such observation, although not the intended yield of the questionnaire, nonetheless deserves mention in the report.

CHAPTER 7

Drawing Conclusions

The context is analyzed and data gathered. Now what? This chapter addresses the complicated question of how to integrate data to answer referral questions. Good clinicians eventually become masterful at the task of integrating data through practice, experience, and, most important, through supervision and consultation with colleagues. There are no shortcuts for any of these. However, to help the learning process along and to give new clinicians and those wanting to improve their skills a starting point, we present a step-by-step guide to integrating data. The process may seem awkward and unwieldy, especially at first, but the steps can be worked through very quickly and, with practice, they become automatic.

We'll use the case of Margaret, the elderly woman introduced in the first chapter, to introduce the steps. As a reminder, Margaret's physician, Dr. Shaw, referred her for an assessment of dementia and its impact on her day-to-day functioning. To conduct the assessment, the psychologist reviewed Margaret's medical records, interviewed Margaret and her son, administered subtests of the Wechsler Adult Intelligence Scale-Third Edition (WAIS-III) and Wechsler Memory Scale-Third Edition (WMS-III), and administered the Beck Depression Inventory-Second Edition (BDI-II). Thus, the psychologist had seven sources of information to interpret and integrate: record review, interview of Margaret, interview of Margaret's son, behavioral observations, WAIS-III, WMS-III, and BDI-II results. To complete the assessment, she defined its focus, used the assessment findings to examine Margaret's functioning, and looked for disparities and incidental findings in the data. Finally, she answered the implicit and explicit referral questions and developed recommendations to improve Margaret's functioning and quality of life.

(Note that information about Margaret is not intended to serve as a guide to conducting an assessment for dementia in an elderly person. Rather, it is offered for illustrative purposes only, to demonstrate stepwise procedures for integrating assessment data. For much more detailed information about assessing dementia in the elderly and differentiating it from depression, see Storandt & VandenBos's [1994] text on the assessment of dementia in older adults.)

Find the Focus

The focus of the assessment is the reason for conducting it. Somebody hired a psychologist to find out something about a client, perhaps to find out if she

- is eligible for special education services;
- needs treatment for a mental health or emotional disorder;
- needs residential placement;
- has mental retardation;
- has a psychotic disorder;
- has a personality disorder, mood disorder, or both;
- has a learning disability or attention-deficit disorder; or
- has dementia.

To find the focus, return to the context questions about the implicit and explicit reasons for referral, and add in information learned about the client thus far in the assessment process. For a patient referred by his psychiatrist for an assessment of schizophrenia, the focus might be on diagnosis but it is also likely to be on treatment recommendations or on addressing the client's long-standing noncompliance with treatment. For the child referred for assessment of reading problems, the focus might be on identifying the source of the reading difficulties and how best to address them, or it might be on determining her eligibility for special education services, or both. At this stage in the assessment, it is essential that the focus be made clear. If it is not, review the context questions, go back to the referral source, and clarify why the assessment is needed or how it can be helpful.

For Margaret, the focus of the assessment is on identifying dementia and, if she has dementia, identifying the impact it has on her day-to-day functioning. Both issues are important for Margaret and her family.

> ### Sidebar 7.1
>
> **Steps to Integrate Data**
>
> Find the focus → Identify domains of functioning → Organize and integrate data → Deal with disparities → Deal with incidental findings → Answer referral questions → Develop recommendations

Identify the Domains of Functioning

In the previous chapter, we defined the concept "domains of functioning" and discussed how to identify the domains that need to be assessed in an individual case. In the information-gathering phase of the assessment, the clinician is both far-reaching and detailed in his assessment. Many narrowly defined domains are identified: Does Sandra have a family history of mental illness? Does she have learning problems? Does she get along well with other people? Does she exercise self-control?

For the integrative stage of assessment, domains identified in the information-gathering phase are consolidated. Some are left out and others combined. The resulting domains are broad and inclusive. They allow the clinician to structure information so that patterns of data can be analyzed for the purpose of understanding and solving a problem. Fortunately, it is not necessary to reinvent the relevant domains in each case, because five domains cover virtually all aspects of functioning that concern psychologists: (1) behavioral functioning, (2) emotional functioning, (3) cognitive functioning, (4) interpersonal functioning, and (5) self-concept. Additional domains (to make the task manageable, not more than one or two) can be added to these as needed.

Organize and Integrate the Data

To complete the task of drawing conclusions from assessment findings, the clinician must pull information about each domain from test findings, interviews, record reviews, and behavioral observations, keeping in mind the focus of the assessment. The clinician does not need to know *everything* about each domain, but he needs to know as much as he can that is relevant to the focus of the assessment, mining the data for information. To be successful, he needs to be knowledgeable about the problem being assessed and the interpretation of test, observational, and interview data. He also must have strong critical thinking and reasoning skills. The clinician must know, for example, what pattern of test results is consistent with dementia, reading disability, depression, thought disorder, or whatever the issue is, or he must review the literature or access supervision or consultation to find out. The clinician must also take into consideration the reliability and validity of the data. At this stage of the assessment process, the clinician must have the background knowledge and the reasoning skills to select important data points and make sense of their patterns.

> **Sidebar 7.2**
>
> **The Five Domains of Functioning**
>
> Five domains cover virtually all aspects of functioning that concern psychologists:
>
> 1. Behavioral functioning
> 2. Emotional functioning
> 3. Cognitive functioning
> 4. Interpersonal functioning
> 5. Self-concept
>
> Additional domains (to make the task manageable, not more than one or two) can be added to these as needed.

Organizing and integrating the data are completed in a series of steps. At the end of the process, the data are organized into a grid with the domains on one axis and tests and procedures on the other, allowing the clinician to read down the grid to find out what was learned about each domain.

How is the grid formed? *First,* create a blank grid appropriate to the case, with the relevant domains on the top (*X*-axis) and the tests and procedures on the left side (*Y*-axis). (For an example, see Table 7.1.) In listing procedures, include interviews, behavioral observations (made during the interview and test administration), and record review separately, so that nothing is left out. Write the referral questions or focus of the assessment on the top, as a visual reminder. *Second,* pull from each test, technique, or procedure information that is relevant to each domain and note it in the appropriate box. Think, "What did I learn about Sandra's behavior from Minnesota Multiphasic Personality Inventory (MMPI-2) results? What did I learn about Sandra's behavior from my observations of her?" and so forth. Not

Table 7.1 Sample Grid

	Behavioral Functioning	Cognitive Functioning	Emotional Functioning	Interpersonal Functioning	Self-Concept	Domain 1	Domain 2
Interview with client							
Interview with informant							
Behavioral observations							
Record review							
Test 1							
Test 2							
Test 3							
Test 4							

every test provides information about every domain, so there will be a number of empty boxes in the grid. *Third,* review the boxes under each domain. There will be findings that are consistent, the same or similar in each box, and findings that are unique. Some of the unique findings are of minor importance and can be ignored. Others are noteworthy and need further examination. (Making this distinction is where reasoning and experience come in. If you are uncertain about the importance of a finding, discuss it with a colleague or supervisor.) Cross out the findings that can be ignored and highlight those that need attention. *Fourth,* at the bottom of the grid, summarize the findings for each domain, highlighting unique findings that need further examination. These we call disparities or incidental findings. Disparities are inconsistencies in the data. Incidental findings are those that are unexpected and not directly relevant to the referral question but important for the client.

Table 7.2 is a completed grid for Margaret. Sample grids for other hypothetical clients are in the appendix.

Deal With Disparities

Margaret's case is fairly simple because there are no disparities in the data. Another "easy" example is a 10-year-old who is not doing well academically and is referred for an educational evaluation. The focus is on why is he not doing well and what will help him be more successful in school. Processing speed and working memory deficits are apparent on cognitive ability testing; fluency deficits show up in achievement testing; there are numerous signs and symptoms of ADHD on behavior rating scales; and there is a family history of ADHD. Again, all the data point to the same conclusions. Or a psychotherapy patient presents with a depressed mood and irritable affect, reports the signs and symptoms of depression, has a family history of depression, and produces a Personality Assessment Inventory (PAI) profile that is positive for depression. It is not difficult to draw conclusions in these situations because in each, the multiple sources of data produce consistent results. However, such cases in many ways are atypical of assessment clients, many of whom present confusing symptom pictures and conflicting test results. For example, Jonathan seems bright and capable, and he is doing well at school. However, at home, he is morose and uncooperative, and he picks fights with his older siblings. Self-report data from testing is all in the normal range, but projective test results hint at a mood disorder, and there is a strong family history of depression. Eliza has not shown improvement despite a long history of treatment for depression. Test results suggest both mood problems and a possible personality disorder, and interview data suggest that she may be motivated to remain ill because she is fearful of returning to work. Ana's parents feel certain that she has ADHD, but her therapist is not sure and thinks that there may be other factors behind her persistent behavior problems. Her test results are not typical of students who have ADHD.

In addition, inconsistencies in test findings, observations, or other data points are prevalent in assessment regardless of client issues for a number of reasons:

Table 7.2   Sample Grid: Margaret

	Behavioral Functioning	Cognitive Functioning	Emotional Functioning	Interpersonal Functioning	Self-Concept	Domain 1: Physical Health
Interview with client	Says everything is OK, except can't find her things	Confused/doesn't know why she's here	Anxious	Pleasant and cooperative	Likes to read, visit friends	
Interview with informant (son)	Poor self-care, food in house is spoiled/very independent and high functioning in the past	Doesn't remember what she's told	Always nervous when she goes out (this is a new problem)	Isolative (new problem), active social life even as a widow, until a couple of years ago		
Behavioral observations	Good manners, pleasant, nervous with testing	Confusion is evident	Nervous	Polite, tries to be cooperative		
Record review (medical records)	Change in functioning in the past 2 years	Confusion during physical exam	Anxious (increase from previous visits)	Always polite and cooperative		In good health, chronic problems are well managed

	Behavioral Functioning	Cognitive Functioning	Emotional Functioning	Interpersonal Functioning	Self-Concept	Domain 1: Physical Health
Test 1 (WAIS-III)		Vocabulary/information above average; digit span/arithmetic; digit symbol less than average				
Test 2 (WMS-III)		All scores less than average based on age-appropriate norms				
Test 3 (BD-I)			In normal range with age-appropriate norms			
Summary	Deterioration from high level of functioning in the past 2 years	Multiple signs of mild dementia	Anxious with new experiences and being out of the house (new problem), no signs of depression	Polite, pleasant, isolative, had active social life in the past	Sense of self and realities of life are discordant	In good health

- Tests that sound the same measure different things. For example, depression as measured on a self-report test is a different construct than depression measured on the Rorschach. There are often differences between findings on implicit (projective), or performance-based, and explicit, or self-report-based, tests (see Ganellen, 2007) because the client cannot or will not report characteristics about herself that are apparent in implicit assessments, such as the Rorschach. For example, an individual in a court-ordered evaluation denies feeling depressed and produces a normal profile on the PAI, but Rorschach data indicate that she has a proneness to depression, limited coping skills, and low self-esteem.

- Data might be inaccurate. The client may be a poor reader or he may have been distracted while taking a self-report test, so that results of a certain scale or subtest are invalid. Also, a certain level of measurement error or randomness in the data is not unexpected and is accounted for in test scoring. Composite scores are stronger measures than subtest-scaled scores, and differences between scores need to be statistically significant to be considered meaningful.

- For interview data, an informant may provide unreliable information because the information he has is inaccurate or because he is purposely misleading.

- The syndrome under consideration might have an inconsistent impact. For example, a student who has ADHD may be exceptionally motivated to do well on certain working memory tests but not others, so results of tests of working memory are inconsistent.

- On behavior rating scales, there may be differences between self and observer ratings or the ratings of two different observers, such as a father and mother, because the individuals completing the rating scales see things differently (see Conners, 2003). Or there may be differences in ratings between observers from different settings, such as school and home, because of differences in the student's behavior in the settings.

- The client may have taken medication one testing day but not the next, or he may have a cold or be very tired from a poor night's sleep. Any of these factors can affect the validity of test results.

To deal with disparities, we recommend the following:

- *Throw out "bad" data:* How do you know if data are "bad," that is, unreliable or invalid? If one data point is inconsistent with all the others and inconsistent with behavioral and situational referents, it may not be reliable. For example, a student obtains a "2" on the Symbol Search subtest of the Wechsler Intelligence Scale for Children-Fourth Edition (WISC-IV). Her other scores are all 7 or above, and she scored in the average range on two other measures of processing speed. In looking closely at the results, it becomes apparent that she made an unusual number of errors on Symbol Search. Does she have difficulty with quick visual scanning of this type or did she make errors for some other reason? Often, there is no way of knowing. It would be a mistake to give too much weight to this one score, when it varies so much with all the other scores and with all the relevant behavioral referents. On the other hand, it is important to be cautious when deciding whether or not to ignore inconsistent data. Err on the side of caution, and note anomalous (inconsistent) data in the written report, indicating either that reasons for the anomaly are unclear, or, if appropriate, that the score is thought to be invalid.

• *Know what tests measure, and how they measure it:* What kinds of information does a test reveal? For example, a cognitive ability test measures verbal and spatial reasoning and language development, while a reading fluency test measures reading speed. The MMPI-2 measures manifest self-reported symptoms and managed impressions, while the Rorschach measures personality organization and dynamics at a less conscious level (Meyer et al., 2001).

• *Develop inferences from patterns of data:* Cognitive ability and reading fluency tests would be expected to covary in a student without noted learning difficulties who has had age-appropriate educational experiences. They might diverge in a student who has a reading disorder or deficits in processing speed, or in a student who has not had much reading practice or gaps in his education. The client who shows signs of depression on the Rorschach and produces a "normal" MMPI-2 profile might have an "underlying depression" that he manages quite well in structured and controlled circumstances.

• *Use the research literature to make sense of disparate findings:* How do gaps in education affect reading scores in students of average intelligence? Are scores on the PAI Depression scale and the BDI-II expected to covary? In what circumstances are differences between subtest-scaled scores on the WISC-IV meaningful?

• *Pay attention to behavioral referents and situational factors:* For example, a client undergoing a social security disability evaluation might be malingering, while a client undergoing a child custody evaluation is going to do his or her best to give a positive impression.

• *Don't feel obligated to make definitive conclusions out of inconsistent data:* Ideally, each assessment yields a clear-cut conclusion supported uniformly by all sources of data. But when the data produced by an assessment are very ambiguous or contradictory, it is not the psychologist's duty to force it all to "make sense." In fact, doing so could misrepresent the actual test results. As unsatisfying as it might be to psychologist and referral source alike, a conclusion that acknowledges confusing or puzzling test results, rather than smoothing them over with definite but unsupported interpretations, might be unavoidable in some cases.

Below is an example about how to handle disparities in test data, based on a hypothetical juvenile court evaluation.

Jeanine is a 15-year-old arrested for the second time on charges of disorderly conduct following aggressive and destructive behavior at home. She rarely leaves the house and spends most of her time in her room listening to music, sleeping, or watching television (*behavioral referents based on clinical interview data*). An evaluation was conducted to make recommendations to the court about a disposition for the case (*the focus of the evaluation, and an important situational factor*). Jeanine produces a valid BASC-2 self-report test that has no significant elevations, in other words, a "normal" profile (*the BASC-2 is a self-report or explicit assessment*). Her mother states Jeanine doesn't listen to her at home, she has been threatening her younger siblings, and she is almost always irritable (*behavioral referents based on informant interview data*). The examiner also notes Jeanine's irritability and low frustration tolerance during the testing session (*behavioral referents based on behavioral observations*). Jeanine shrugged her shoulder when asked about her problems, and she went on to deny having any troubles or concerns (*clinical interview data*). Results of projective drawings, a sentence completion test, and the Thematic Apperception Test hint at depression and low self-esteem, and Rorschach results indicate a high level of defensiveness and the presence of overwhelmingly painful emotions when emotional demands are placed on her (*performance-based, projective, or implicit assessment*). Jeanine has functioned poorly at school and at home since she entered middle school, despite strong family support and periodic efforts at treatment (*behavioral referents based on record review*).

What are the disparities in the data? Self-report and child interview data suggest that nothing's wrong. On a self-report test and during an interview, Jeanine portrayed herself as being free of problems. In contrast, all the other data, including multiple behavioral and situational referents, indicate that Jeanine is extremely irritable, flies into destructive rages, and is socially withdrawn. The data point to a mood disorder. Are the disparities due to obviously invalid or unreliable data? No, Jeanine produced valid profiles on all tests. What do the conflicting tests measure? The self-report test measures Jeanine's view of herself; projective tests may assess information that is out of Jeanine's awareness or that she chooses not to portray.

What inferences can be drawn from reviewing the disparities in the data? Jeanine might not recognize or have words to describe her problems, or she may purposefully deny problems to affect the outcome of the evaluation. Is it possible that Jeanine is right and her mother, test results, and records are wrong? This is not likely, because the behavioral referents as documented in a police report and in school, probation, and treatment records indicate that Jeanine has significant behavior problems.

The clinician concludes that Jeanine very likely has an underlying depression and related irritability and that these are the primary factors behind her behavior problems. He recommends follow-up mental health treatment to address depression, related family problems, and Jeanine's behavior problems. He also recommends probation requirements to cooperate with treatment. The clinician might also address

Jeanine's resistance to treatment, speculating on its source and how best to engage her in the treatment process. However, this goes beyond the focus of the assessment, and the clinician may or may not have information relevant to this point.

Deal With Incidental Findings

Another problem that sometimes comes up in assessment is incidental findings. George is a bright, hardworking boy who is being evaluated for entrance into a gifted and talented middle school program. He takes a battery of achievement tests, and, to everybody's surprise, results suggest that he has a relative weakness in math and may meet criteria for a mathematics disorder (learning disability in math). Juanita lives with her husband and two children, and she has been working at the same job for many years. She took part in an assessment prior to beginning treatment for depression. Results are consistent with depression but also suggest the possibility of an underlying thought disorder.

How should these incidental findings be handled? At the least, they need to be documented and possible behavioral referents explored. Does George have problems learning math? Has he been working much harder than his peers on learning new material? Has he had a tutor or does he go for extra help on a regular basis? Does Juanita have other signs of thought disorder? Does she hear voices? Is there a family history of mental illness? The problem can be monitored, or, if the finding is important, a referral for additional assessment should be considered.

Answer Referral Questions

Using assessment findings to answer referral questions is the heart of the assessment process. Like working a jigsaw puzzle with the pieces sorted out but not yet put together, answering referral questions requires logical thinking and analysis of patterns of data. Every case is unique. At this stage in the assessment process, there are no simple steps to follow to get to the right answer. Rather, the clinician needs to think the problem through, always keeping in mind the focus of the assessment. Below are examples of the thought process used to answer referral questions at three levels: simple, moderate, and complex.

Simple

Marisa was referred for evaluation to determine if she has a reading disorder and if she is eligible for academic support and accommodations at college. Scores on reading achievement tests are significantly below expectations relative to her cognitive ability, and she has a long history of reading problems. The answers to the referral questions are obvious. Marisa has a reading disorder and should be eligible for academic support and accommodations.

Moderate

Allen is a 12-year-old boy in the seventh grade. He has been acting out in class, and his teachers ask his parents to agree to an evaluation for learning and attention problems. There are a number of indicators of ADHD on testing and on behavior rating scales, but Allen also shows signs of an expressive language disorder, and he reports significant family problems as well. The examiner concludes that he should have additional speech and language evaluations and recommends that he work with the school counselor on stress management. She remains uncertain about ADHD and recommends reevaluation in a year if the problems continue. She also makes recommendations to minimize Allen's acting out behavior in class, since this was the problem that resulted in the referral.

Complex

Danny, age 22, was referred for evaluation by his therapist for two reasons: He wanted to return to college and needed to access academic support and accommodations due to emotional problems, and he had long-standing problems with anxiety that had not responded to medication or psychotherapy. Danny was a complicated young man, extremely bright and talented, extremely dependent and immature, and severely traumatized from abuse he suffered in childhood. The focus of the assessment became how to help him succeed in school and how best to treat and manage his depression and anxiety symptoms. The examiner administered a battery of cognitive, achievement, projective, and self-report tests and had a good sense of his functioning, which was erratic, across several domains. Results indicated that he had periodic problems with attention and concentration, bouts of depression, and a tendency toward agoraphobia and public-speaking anxiety, all of which would affect his school experience. The examiner was able to formulate some ideas about early childhood and more immediate precipitants to his depression and anxiety symptoms and treatment strategies that might help. She also addressed problems and obstacles in the therapy and how to move past them. Finally, she recommended specific support and accommodations that could be provided at school.

As might be evident from the examples, every case is unique. To answer referral questions, follow these steps: gather information, find the focus of the assessment, and mine the data for what is relevant to each domain of functioning. Then use good logic and reasoning skills to draw accurate and relevant conclusions. Even in complex cases, if the questions are posed well and the data collected appropriately, the answers are almost always present. They just need to be illuminated.

Some guidelines to keep in mind:

• Sometimes less is more. Take out information that is not important and focus on the major issues or concerns.

• Pay attention to situational factors. Assessment findings are about an individual, but the individual is part of a family and lives and works with other people. Individual issues are often only a small part of a larger, more complex picture. Even so, the examiner does not have to know everything about the situation to provide useful information.

- In rare circumstances, assessment findings do not provide an answer to referral questions, and the examiner is left with the frustrating conclusion that he doesn't know and can't find out the answer to the question.

- An assessment is not a crystal ball; it cannot predict the future. It is an imperfect but often powerful method to learn about a person and his problems and strengths.

Develop Recommendations

Recommendations are expected at the end of most assessments and should follow naturally from the clinician's conclusions. Helpful recommendations require knowledge about the problem or condition being assessed. This kind of knowledge is gained from didactic instruction, the research literature, experience, and supervision. They also require knowledge of child and adult development and knowledge of resources in the community and in the larger world (e.g., professional services, books, Web sites, or organizations that might be helpful). In addition, helpful recommendations require good reasoning skills and good judgment—not clinical judgment, but everyday judgment. And finally, they require good communication skills.

Recommendations should obviously address referral problems, but they should also address other problems that become apparent in the course of the assessment. While addressing the problems, they need to take into account contextual factors relevant to the case, especially the audience for the report and systems issues. The psychologist needs to be mindful and accepting of realistic limitations. In most situations, it is best to work with systems and services that are readily available, even if they are not ideal; otherwise, recommendations run the risk of being rejected. However, when readily available solutions to a problem are inhumane or unethical, the psychologist might (and perhaps in some instances, must) advocate for services that are more difficult to access. In such circumstances, well-developed recommendations that follow directly from a thorough assessment can be powerful tools for advocacy.

An often neglected aspect of making recommendations is the not infrequent need to refer for additional assessments by professionals in other areas. A referral to a physician might be appropriate for a client who is unusually lethargic, while a recommendation for a vision exam may be needed when a client has trouble with visual processing tasks. Schoolchildren are often referred to a speech pathologist to evaluate language or auditory-processing disorders or to an occupational therapist for difficulty with fine motor skills or coordination problems. It is a good idea to explore what other specialists are available and what they do, in order to make effective recommendations for additional assessments as needed.

One way to think through possible recommendations is to review the problem's impact on day-to-day functioning, using the five domains described above. Joanne is a bright girl who has a reading disability along with related anxiety and low self-esteem (cognitive, emotional, self-concept domains). She is shy and avoids reading aloud in the classroom (behavioral domain). She prefers to stay inside at recess and does not interact easily with classmates (behavioral, interpersonal domains). How should her reading disability be addressed at school and at home? What other interventions would be helpful to Joanne? Gwen is a teenager who is mildly mentally retarded (cognitive domain). She has a number of behavior problems and, recently, while hanging around with some other girls, she was arrested for disorderly conduct (behavior, interpersonal domains). She offers no complaints (self-concept, emotional domains). What could help Gwen manage her behavior better?

The following are guidelines for developing recommendations:

- Be realistic and practical.

- Be specific, but not so specific that the recommendation constrains the audience for the report unnecessarily.

- Do not make recommendations outside of your area of expertise. Be mindful and respectful of professional boundaries.

- Make recommendations that are appropriate to the referral source and the audience.

- Cover all bases, the problem outlined in the referral and others that come up in the assessment.

- Anticipate problems and address them.

- Don't use the assessment report as a "soapbox." Focus on the one client and how to best meet his needs.

- Prioritize recommendations.

- If recommendations are vital to risk management, safety, or other major concerns, highlight them. If there are imminent concerns about risk, tell somebody who is in a position to do something about it. (Limits to confidentiality should always be discussed with clients at the outset of the assessment as part of the informed consent process. This process will be covered in greater detail in Chapter 10.)

APPENDIX: HYPOTHETICAL CLIENTS

Sample Grid: John

	Behavioral Functioning	Cognitive Functioning	Emotional Functioning	Interpersonal Functioning	Self-Concept	Domain 1	Domain 2
Interview with client	Says he gets in trouble with his teacher	Says he is a good speller and good at math	Denies sadness, admits to getting mad	Says he has lots of friends, likes to play with them	Frustrated with self		
Interview with informant (mother)	Very active since toddler years	Parents are attorneys; learns quickly if interested	Cheerful except when thwarted	Loves playing with other kids; has fun	Tells mom, "I'm no good at . . . ."		
Behavioral observations	Plays and moves around as he talks, short attention span	Figures things out quickly when playing; makes connections	Seems happy except when frustrated or thwarted	Friendly and engaging; very talkative			
Record review (report card)	Teacher: behavior problems (e.g., out of seat) in class, lunch, recess	Keeps up with classmates, does well when interested	"Cheerful boy"	"Very social," "talks to peers while teacher is talking"	Increasingly frustrated in class		

(Continued)

(Continued)

	Behavioral Functioning	Cognitive Functioning	Emotional Functioning	Interpersonal Functioning	Self-Concept	Domain 1	Domain 2
Test 1 (CPRS/CTRS)	Hyperactive behavior at home and at school? Opposition	Inattentive at home, not at school	Per mother, mildly psychosomatic? Anxiety	Hyperactive, fidgety			
Test 2 (WISC-IV)		Verbal and performance > average; WMI and PSI < average					
Test 3 (TAT/drawing)	Impulse control problems/excitable	Can do complex work if interested and not fatigued	Frustrated, not anxious; playful and cheerful	Positive attachment to family	Impulsivity/high activity level is egosyntonic?		
Test 4 Summary	Short attention span/hyperactive/impulsive	Bright but low frustration tolerance; does well when interested	Cheerful except when frustrated	Good relationships but overly talkative; hyperactivity interferes	Frustration affecting self-concept; also likes his high energy, high activity level		

Sample Grid: Jeanine

	Behavioral Functioning	Cognitive Functioning	Emotional Functioning	Interpersonal Functioning	Self-Concept	Family History?	Substance Abuse? Trauma History
Interview with client	Denies having any problems	Denies learning problems	Denies depression; other emotional problems	Says she has lots of friends			Denies both
Interview with informant (mother)	J. is uncooperative; threatens sister; irritable; isolative	Used to be a good student	J. is very angry; J. is always in a bad mood	Used to have nice friends, but not social in last year	Used to do a lot of activities and was proud of accomplish-ments	Positive family history depression (maternal grandmother) and substance abuse (father's side)	No known trauma, don't know about SA
Behavioral observations	Irritable! unmotivated, apathetic	Seems slowed	Depressed, angry; blunted affect when not irritable	Unfriendly, hard to engage, minimal cooperation	Down on self? Self-hating? Righteous indignation		
Record review	Disorderly conduct charge × 2; suspended from school × 2 for fighting; truant	Used to be a good student	Probation officer finds her depressed	Difficult to engage; marginally cooperative			Negative drug screens

(Continued)

(Continued)

	Behavioral Functioning	Cognitive Functioning	Emotional Functioning	Interpersonal Functioning	Self-Concept	Family History?	Substance Abuse? Trauma History
Test 1 (BASC-2)	Valid profile		No evidence of depression, anxiety, other emotional problems	Reports satisfying relationships	Normal profile; does not admit to problems		
Test 2 (WISC-IV)	Low motivation/likely underestimate	All scores low average to average	Slowed processing speed?	Apathetic			
Test 3 (Projectives)	Defensive, minimal productions		Underlying painful emotions; problems of depression with hopelessness	Disengaged, withdrawn; angry at world	Self-contempt?		
Summary	Irritable, unmotivated, defensive, history of aggressive behavior? Loss of control	Average intellect affected by depression mood?	Underlying depression is highly probable? Suicide risk due to hopelessness/anger	Withdrawn from peers and family, but denies	Likely negative feelings about self and others	Depression in maternal grandmother	No evidence of SA, but should be monitored

CHAPTER 8

Form and Content of the Assessment Report

D r. Greene is frustrated. She spent hours writing an assessment report about Amanda, a fourth-grade student at her school. Amanda was falling behind in her schoolwork and misbehaving in class. Her teacher and parents agreed that she should be evaluated by Dr. Greene, the school psychologist. They wanted to understand why Amanda's grades were poor and why she was misbehaving.

Dr. Greene reviewed Amanda's school records and interviewed Amanda, her teacher, and her parents. She administered the WISC-IV, behavior-rating scales, and projective tests. In her report, she carefully recorded the background information, her observations, and test results along with her tentative conclusions about Amanda's learning and behavior problems and some recommendations about how to support her academic achievement and minimize her behavior problems in the classroom. She sent the report several days in advance to all who were scheduled to be present at a meeting about Amanda. At the meeting, Dr. Greene's conclusions were reviewed and she was asked her opinion about what to do. Dr. Greene was left wondering why she had spent hours carefully recording information and making her report clear and easy to follow. She thought, "Why not just list the scores and write a few lines about my conclusions and recommendations? I could have saved myself a lot of time."

Psychologists who work in all kinds of settings have the same concerns. The psychologist who evaluates psychiatric inpatients might hear from the treating psychiatrist that he would prefer her reports to be written like medical reports, with a page or two of data followed by brief conclusions. A psychologist in a forensic setting might have his report discarded because it does not support the case the attorney is making for her client. A psychologist evaluating a client referred by her therapist because of concerns about psychotic thinking might find that her report is quickly reviewed and filed away as soon as the question is answered.

Why should Dr. Greene and other psychologists spend time laboring over reports if they are not thoughtfully reviewed? What purpose does the psychological assessment report serve? What information should be included in it, and what can be left out? How should it be organized?

Form

Psychological assessment reports serve two important and distinct functions: communication and documentation. The report provides information about the psychologist's procedures, observations, and findings, and typically it becomes part of a legal, educational, or medical record. The information is presented to the primary audience for the report and may also be presented to secondary audiences, perhaps years later. The report is also, in most instances, made available to the client or his parents. For example, a school psychologist might write a report to present at a meeting of a student's parents, teachers, and administrators. The information is to be used to determine the student's eligibility for special education services and to plan an educational program for her. The report becomes part of the student's confidential special education record and will likely be reviewed as the student progresses in school. A clinical psychologist working in a psychiatric hospital might write a report to communicate information to treatment team members and case managers about a patient's diagnosis and personality functioning and to make recommendations for treatment. The report becomes part of the patient's medical record, and years later it could be accessed, with the patient's permission, by her therapist or an attorney. A forensic psychologist might write a report addressing a client's competence to stand trial. The report becomes part of a legal record. Keeping the function of the report and its possible trajectory in mind at the outset helps the psychologist find the right structure or form for the report. Also, the need to write the report with care becomes apparent.

For many psychologists the process of preparing a report allows them to better understand the client and her needs. Writing helps clarify thinking; for example, defining jargon helps the writer understand the concept behind it.

In any assessment situation, decisions about the format for the report and about what to include in the report and what to leave out should be determined by the functions the report will serve. A case-focused report, one that "centers on the specific problems outlined by the referring person" (Groth-Marnat, 1999, p. 619) is the most appropriate for the types of problems we have been discussing. A report that serves a gatekeeping, administrative, or forensic function needs to include information that allows its conclusions to be disputed, such as detailed test scores and their interpretations. Reports in this category are focused on such issues as the need for academic accommodations, eligibility for special programs or services, waivers of requirements, competency to stand trial, custody and visitation plans, liability in personal injury claims, or criminal responsibility. Reports that serve clinical or educational functions, such as differential diagnosis, treatment planning, or educational planning, do not have to include information that would allow findings to be disputed. If he is not in agreement with its conclusions, the client requesting the report can simply ignore them or obtain a second opinion. However, the kind of information included in the report affects its persuasiveness, and the more persuasive the report the more likely its findings will have an impact.

Settings or systems that refer clients for assessment, such as schools, agencies, or clinics, typically require reports to be prepared in a specific format. In most instances, the formats are suitable and make it easier for the psychologist to complete his work. However, it is the psychologist's responsibility, as the writer of the report, to ensure that the report format is appropriate for its function. Also, from time to time, the psychologist might need to create a format for a report to suit a specific assessment situation.

The following are real-world examples of report formats used in different settings, with each bullet point representing the heading of a distinct section of the report. Note that these are only examples. Every court, school district, clinic, agency, and so forth could have its own unique format.

Forensic reports for legal setting (based on reports submitted to Connecticut Juvenile Courts; A. Campagna, personal communication, March 31, 2007):

- Identifying information
- Circumstances of referral
- Date and nature of clinical contacts
- Collateral data sources
- Relevant background information
- Clinical findings
- Psychological-legal formulation

Psychological assessment reports for the public schools (based on a report model for East Lyme, Connecticut, Public Schools; S. Buck, personal communication, February 4, 2007):

- Identifying information (including the name of the school, the teacher, test dates, and referral source)
- Reason for referral
- Tests or assessment procedures
- Background information/interview/present academic functioning
- Behavioral observations
- Test results
- Discussion

A report for a clinical setting; for example, to submit to the client's therapist (Kvaal, Choca, & Groth-Marnat, 2003):

- Identifying information
- Reason for referral
- Presenting complaints
- Procedures

- Background information
- Behavioral observations and mental status examination
- Test results
- Discussion
- Diagnostic impressions
- Summary and recommendations (pp. 418–425)

As is evident, the formats overlap quite a bit, but they are based on the specific needs they serve. All reports, regardless of setting, should include information about the reason for referral, procedures, results (along with a validity statement), and conclusions. The purpose of including this information in a report is to allow a secondary audience to make sense of it. For example, a report listing test findings and presenting the conclusion that the patient is not a suicide risk, without additional contextual, validity, and procedural information, could be confusing and misleading to a secondary audience. Adding the additional information provides the context for making sense of it.

In developing a format for reports, keep in mind these goals: The format should be logical and easy for the reader to follow. It should conform to audience expectations. It must communicate results in a way that meets ethical standards (see Chapter 10). It must have a place for all necessary information. Finally, the format should make it easier for the psychologist to write the report. Headings, tables, and a numbering system (for a list of recommendations) make a report more manageable, because such devices organize complex material for the reader and so make the material easier to understand. Also, the reader can look back through the report to find specific information, as needed. These devices also make it easier for the psychologist to prepare the report, because they provide a convenient organizational structure.

Sidebar 8.2

Developing a Report Format

When creating a new report format, make sure the structure

- is logical and easy for the reader to follow,
- conforms to audience expectations,
- meets legal and ethical standards (see Chapter 10),
- has a place for all necessary information, and
- makes it easy for the psychologist to write the report.

Content

Once the format is determined, the psychologist decides what information to include in each section of the report and what to leave out. It is useful to consider the following questions in making these decisions:

- What does the reader need to know?
- What might the reader want to know?
- What information does the psychologist want the reader to have in order to support his findings and recommendations?
- What information stands out, even if it doesn't fit in?
- What information paints a picture, allowing the reader to "know" a client?

Below are guidelines for what should be included in each section of the report, along with examples. Note that there is more than one way to write an effective assessment report. (The examples are included to illustrate the content of each section of the report; they are not intended as models of best practices in writing style, a topic covered extensively in Chapter 9).

Identifying Information

In this section, include, at least, name (also, nicknames or aliases, other names the client goes by, possibly former names, such as maiden names, as well), date of birth (useful in distinguishing between two individuals with the same name), and the date of the evaluation or report.

Name: John Doe

Date of birth: 12/20/00

Date of report: 02/29/08

Reason for Referral

In this section, include the name, job function, or agency affiliation of the individual making the referral or all three, and state the goals or purpose of the assessment as clearly as possible.

> John Doe was referred for psychological evaluation by Dr. Jean Smith, his pediatrician, following a routine physical exam. Dr. Smith asked that John be evaluated for ADHD and depression, and she also asked for treatment recommendations.

Procedures

The goal of this section is to inform the reader about the exact procedures that were completed and that led to the report's conclusions. List all procedures, including interviews, specific observation periods (such as classroom observation), record reviews (list the records that were reviewed, and, depending on the purpose of the report, additional identifying details), tests that were administered, and tests that were attempted. When listing tests, it is customary to write out the formal name of the test (e.g., Wechsler Intelligence Scale for Children-Fourth Edition or WISC-IV) and follow it with initials, in parentheses, that will later be used in writing about the tests. Other useful information, such as which form of the test was administered, is also included within the parentheses, after the initials.

Clinical Interview

Classroom Observation (11:30–12:00 2/24/08)

Parent Interview (with mother)

Record Review (school progress reports; medical records)

Conners' Parent Rating Scale Revised-Long form (CPRS; mother's report)

Conners' Teacher Rating Scale Revised-Short form (CTRS; classroom teacher and literacy teacher)

Wechsler Intelligence Scale for Children-Fourth Edition (WISC-IV)

Kinetic Family Drawing

Thematic Apperception Test (TAT; selected cards)

Note that for forensic reports and some that have an administrative focus, very specific details about procedures should be included, so that the reader knows the precise information the examiner used in drawing his conclusions. Also note that the above is *not* meant to be a recommended battery of tests to assess ADHD and depression in a 7-year-old.

Background Information

The background information section includes information about situational factors and the client's history and comes primarily from records and interviews. This section serves a number of purposes. It helps the psychologist build a case for his findings, provides readers with the information the psychologist drew on in forming her conclusions, and helps readers know the client. The information included in this section varies considerably according to the purpose of the report, the information that is available, and the preferences of the psychologist.

Information in this section should be relevant to referral questions and based on facts rather than opinions. For example, "According to Mrs. Smith, Jonah does not get along with his brothers," could have a place in the background section, while the statement, "In Ms. Smith's opinion, Jonah fights with his brothers because his father neglects him," belongs in a section reporting interview data. The latter is an editorial comment that could be quite biased; the former is closer to a statement of fact in that it could be verified. In this case, the statement's accuracy is maintained by including the first few words, "According to Ms. Smith . . . ."

It is important for the psychologist to avoid editorializing in this section and to allow the facts to "speak for themselves." For example, Nathan, a 13-year-old boy with low intellectual functioning, was left unsupervised for most of the day. The psychologist believes that poor supervision contributed to his delinquent behavior. In the background section she writes, among other things, about his poor academic performance and how he spends his time. These facts prepare the reader for the psychologist's opinion, which comes at the end of the report. Including these aspects of Nathan's history in the background section makes the report more persuasive.

In writing the background section, follow either a chronological structure, or one organized by topic, or combine the two structures. A chronological review of background information is organized developmentally, from prenatal experiences through adulthood. A themed approach to background information might include psychiatric history, medical history, social history, educational history, and occupational history (Kvaal et al., 2003), or other topics that are relevant to referral questions. In a combined approach, a developmental or chronological history is supplemented by additional information such as family history of psychiatric disorder or treatment history. Note that a report focusing on a specific problem, such as a child's reading difficulty, should avoid including extraneous information. In contrast, a report addressing broad issues, such as social and emotional functioning, needs to include a wide range of information.

These are some guidelines to follow in deciding what information to include in the background information section of the report and what to leave out:

- Include information in anticipation of reader's questions. For example, if a recommendation is made to place a child in a residential facility, the reader might want to know of previous treatment efforts. On the other hand, leave out information that might simply satisfy a reader's curiosity.

- Include information that helps the reader to "know" the client, to get a picture of her. For a child referred by the court, it is helpful to report his family constellation and living situation, even if his behavior problems occur at school. For a child who has a reading problem, it is helpful to include information about the class she is in and the reading program she is working on.

- Include information that minimizes gaps; that is, include as many of the pieces of the assessment "puzzle" as possible. For example, if the report addresses diagnostic questions, and the diagnosis is one that is often genetically linked, include a family history relevant to the diagnosis. If the report addresses the question of ADHD in an adult, include the childhood academic history.

- Be discreet. The psychologist will gain more information about a client and his family than should be put into a report. If it is not in the best interest of the client for the information to be disclosed, and it is not necessary to disclose it for the purpose of the assessment, then leave it out to protect the client's privacy.

John Doe is a 7-year-old boy who lives in Park Slope with his parents and 5-year-old sister. Both parents are attorneys and all family members are in good health. There are no unusual family stressors.

John was born at full term without complications. He was a healthy baby, and he met early developmental milestones as expected. Mother cared for John at home until she returned to work part-time when he was a year old. Since then he has been cared for by a live-in nanny while mother is at work. Mother reports that John was an extremely active toddler and that he was more active than most of his classmates in preschool. He continues to display a high level of activity in his public school second-grade classroom. According to Mrs. Doe, his teacher has difficulty managing John's behavior in the classroom, but he keeps up with his classmates academically.

(Continued)

(Continued)

Mother reports that John has playmates but often has conflicts with them and is easily provoked. He plays soccer and chess after school in supervised settings. He usually enjoys these activities and is competent at them, but recently he has refused to participate.

There is a positive family history of depression paternally. There is no known trauma history and no history of treatment for emotional or behavior problems.

Behavioral Observations and Mental Status

Observations about behavior contribute to the assessment in three ways: (1) by supplementing test findings, (2) by providing examples of behavior that test findings attempt to explain, and (3) by contributing to judgments about the validity of test results. For example, the psychologist conducting her assessment notes that Joanne speaks slowly and does not make eye contact. Her facial expression is sad, and she is tearful from time to time. Her mood appears to be depressed and her affect, or the manner in which she expresses her mood, is appropriate to the content of her speech. Test results are consistent with a diagnosis of depression. In this case, the behavioral observations and the test results reinforce each other. The findings have more credibility than they would otherwise. Behavioral observations are essential to judgments about the validity of test findings. For example, Jane is attentive to tasks and motivated to do well on testing. The examiner concludes that test results offer a valid estimate of Jane's functioning. If she were inattentive or uncooperative, the examiner might conclude otherwise.

The information included in this section of the report is based on what the psychologist observes about the client's behavior and, in some cases, the client's responses to specific mental status examination questions, such as those concerning her orientation to person, place, and time. The information in this section is descriptive and concrete, although it is often necessary for the psychologist to make judgments about appearance, mannerisms, mood, affect, quality of thinking, and degree of cooperation. Also, a statement is typically included in this section regarding the validity of test findings. The statement is a judgment based on the client's behavior during the assessment.

Topics typically included in this section are as follows:

- Appearance
- Style of interaction/presentation
- Level of cooperation and motivation
- Mood and affect
- Thought process
- Specific mental status concerns, as relevant to the function of the evaluation

Observations are usually reported in paragraph form and contain detailed descriptions. They should be presented in an organized manner, for example, using the sequence appearance, demeanor, cooperation, mood, affect, and, finally, thought process. The level of detail included in the section should be based on the function of the report and the preferences of the psychologist.

> John presented for evaluation as a handsome, friendly boy who appeared his stated age. He was a little disheveled in appearance, with his shirt tucked halfway into his pants, but his hygiene was fine. Although he stopped for introductions, John jumped right into playing noisily with the toys he found in a box on the side of the room. He was able to listen and talk as he played. John was able to work on tasks for about 20 minutes at a time. After that he became irritable and increasingly resistant to task demands. He was not able to come back to a task after a break. Apart from irritability when asked to do something he didn't want to do, he was in good spirits, and he had a bright affect. He talked easily about himself in a brief interview. His thinking was mostly clear and organized, although he was easily distracted and tended to change topics more often than expected. The WISC-IV was completed over two sessions and may underestimate his abilities to a slight extent due to lapses in his motivation and attention to task demands. Also, scores from the WISC-IV may not be stable over time because of John's age.

Test Results and Interpretation

Test scores are derived from a wide range of instruments, including tests of cognitive functioning, memory, other neuropsychological functions, and academic achievement; structured interviews; behavior-rating scales; objective and performance-based (projective) personality tests; and single-construct paper-and-pencil tests. The tests, the scores derived from them, and their interpretation are explained to the reader in this section of the report.

Depending on the purpose of the assessment and the preferences of the psychologist, scores from all administered tests can be included in the narrative of the report or attached to the report in an appendix. Alternatively, the psychologist can report some scores in their entirety and summarize others. It is important to base decisions about which scores to report on the goals of the assessment, not on which scores support the psychologist's conclusions. Scores that don't "fit" need to be explained, not ignored. When a score or a finding is anomalous—that is, when it cannot be explained—the report should note that, too.

Tests of cognitive functioning and academic achievement require low levels of inference for interpretation, and every score from these tests is meaningful. Scores from these tests are typically reported in a test-by-test format, so that all scores are adequately described and interpreted. Personality tests and behavior-rating scales are constructed and interpreted differently than tests of cognitive functioning and academic achievement. For many of these tests, scores in the normal range do not differ from one another in a meaningful way no matter how high or low they are, while scores that are above, or in some cases below, a certain level are noteworthy. The MMPI-2, MCMI-III, PAI, BASC-2, and many behavior-rating scales fall into this category. For these tests, the entire profile of scores can be reported with notations about which scores are elevated and to what level; or, alternatively, normal-range scores can be excluded because they do not offer unique information. Personality tests that are concerned with normal personality dimensions rather than psychopathology, such as the California Psychological Inventory or CPI, are often scored on continuous, dimensional scales. On these tests, scores at moderate levels are meaningful, as are scores at more extreme levels. The scales offer unique information regardless of the score, and all scores should be reported as they are with tests of intellectual functioning.

Test results that require a high level of inference to interpret, including those from performance-based personality (projective) tests such as the Rorschach, are often discussed without referencing specific scores. The scoring systems for these tests are tools the psychologist uses to guide his interpretations. Scores are not meaningful to those who are not knowledgeable about the scoring system, and in most circumstances there is no reason to report them.

Reporting Interpretations of Test Scores and Other Test Data

Writing about the interpretation of low-inference tests such as intelligence and achievement tests is straightforward. Scores are reviewed and interpreted in a logical order, from the general to the specific. Summary scores, including IQ and index scores, are reviewed and categorized (e.g., average, low average, or high average) first, and the meaning of the scores is described; then subtest-scaled scores are reviewed, categorized, and described. Writing about the interpretation of tests relevant to social and emotional functioning and the assessment of personality is much more complex. Psychologists vary in how they approach this task, depending in part on their theoretical orientation. Some psychologists offer test-by-test interpretations, summarizing the data from each test administered and its interpretation. They might include statements such as these:

> MMPI-2 results indicate that Jane is likely to be depressed and distrustful. . . . The BDI-II is consistent with a moderate level of depression. . . . Jane's TAT stories suggest that she struggles with feelings of helplessness and hopelessness.

Other psychologists integrate the data and offer interpretations on a domain-by-domain basis: "Results indicate Jane is likely to struggle with depression and related feelings of hopelessness. She does not trust others, but she is also likely to feel dependent on them."

Reporting interpretations in a test-by-test format is easier to accomplish for the psychologist, but it does not result in a description of the client and his or her struggles and resources. Instead, it results in a poorly organized list of traits, problems, and, sometimes, strengths. Its usefulness is limited (Kvaal et al., 2003). A good alternative is to report interpretations of low-inference test data, typically concerning cognitive functioning, academic achievement, personality features, or problem areas based on objective personality tests (especially when the test score is straightforward to interpret and can add to the persuasiveness of the report), and results of single construct tests (such as the BDI-II) on a test-by-test basis. Then one may write about the client's social and emotional functioning or personality in a domain-by-domain format.

The Conners' scales are behavior-rating scales often used in the diagnosis of ADHD and other behavioral concerns. Two of John's teachers (classroom and literacy) completed the CTRS-Revised (Short Form) and the following scores were obtained:

	T Score	
	Teacher 1	*Teacher 2*
Oppositional	61[a]	53
Cognitive problems/inattention	46	46
Hyperactivity	78[b]	76[b]
Conners' ADHD Index	67[b]	66[b]

a. Possible problem.
b. Significant problem.

Mrs. Doe completed the CPRS (Long Form), producing a valid profile with scaled scores as follows:

	T Score
Oppositional	56
Cognitive problems/inattention	68[a]
Hyperactivity	89[a]
Anxious-shy	43
Perfectionism	47
Social problems	59
Psychosomatic	63
Conners' ADHD Index	74[a]
Conners' Global Index: Restless-impulsive	77[a]
Conners' Global Index: Emotional lability	51
Conners' Global Index: Total	70[a]
DSM-IV: Inattentive	69[a]
DSM-IV: Hyperactive-impulsive	90[a]
DSM-IV: Total	82[a]

a. Significant problem.

Taken together, CTRS and CPRS results indicate that John's behavior is markedly hyperactive at home and at school. Problems with inattention are noted at home, and he may be mildly oppositional at school, depending on the circumstances. Generally, results are consistent with an ADHD diagnosis.

The WISC-IV is a commonly used measure of intellectual functioning in children. It includes several subtests, each measuring a different cognitive ability, and these are combined to form four index scores and the full-scale IQ. John obtained the following scores (mean = 100):

	IQ/Index Score	Percentile	Range (95% CI)
Verbal comprehension (VCI)	114	82	106–120
Perceptual reasoning (PRI)	115	84	106–121
Working memory (WMI)	088	21	081–097
Processing speed (PSI)	085	16	078–096
Full-scale IQ (FSIQ)	105	63	100–110

The VCI and PRI are in the high average range of intellectual functioning relative to his peers. The WMI and PSI are in the low average range, and the FSIQ is in the average range. There are statistically significant differences (at the .05 level) between the following index scores:

	Base Rate (frequency of difference in the standardization sample)
VCI > WMI	03.6
PRI > WMI	04.0
VCI > PSI	03.3
PRI > PSI	02.0

Taken together, results indicate John's verbal and perceptual abilities are above average relative to his peers. His working memory is somewhat below average and weaker than his verbal and perceptual abilities. His processing speed (or quickness in completing routine information-processing tasks) is also somewhat below average and weaker than his verbal and perceptual abilities.

John obtained the following subtest-scaled scores:

Verbal Comprehension	Perceptual Reasoning
Similarities 12	Block design 12
Vocabulary 12	Picture concepts 11
Comprehension 14	Matrix reasoning 14

Working Memory	Processing Speed
Digit Span 07	Coding 07
Letter-Number Sequencing 09	Symbol Search 08

Results indicate that John's verbal reasoning skills and vocabulary are in the average range relative to his peers. His social understanding and judgment are a bit above average. Similarly, his spatial-organization and categorical-reasoning skills are in the average range, while his spatial-reasoning skills are slightly above average. John scored in the average range or close to it on two tests of working memory—one that required him to recall series of digits (going forward and also in reverse order) and another that required him to recall and reorganize a series of numbers and letters. John also scored in the average range or close to it on two tests of processing speed—one that required him to copy symbols associated with numbers and another that required him to scan a text to determine if two symbols were the same or different.

John completed two tests relevant to social and emotional functioning: (1) the Thematic Apperception Technique (TAT; selected cards) and (2) the Kinetic Family Drawing. For the Kinetic Family Drawing, John was asked to draw a picture of his family doing something. John drew a cheerful picture of himself with his parents and brother at an amusement park. He and his father are in one bumper car, and his mother and brother are in another. John is driving and aiming right for his mother's car. Everybody has a wide smile on his or her face. John gave very brief TAT stories, having lost some interest in working at this point in the assessment. With the family drawings, his stories suggest that John struggles with impulsivity and has mixed feelings about it. He worries about the consequences but enjoys the action. Both tests also suggest that he has a positive attachment to family members, ordinary needs for nurturance and affection, and a healthy interest in other people.

Summary and Recommendations

This section should include a brief summary, no more than a few paragraphs at most, of assessment findings based on an integration of background information, observations, and test findings. The summary should address referral questions; it should also anticipate the needs of the audience and provide a "picture" of the client and her problems and strengths. It should be carefully organized so that the points leading up to the conclusions are easy to follow, and recommendations should flow very naturally from the summary statement. Although preparing an effective summary that meets the above goals is not an easy task, it is made manageable by always keeping the function of the report and the needs of the audience in mind. Ask the following questions: Will the information add to the reader's understanding of the client and her troubles? Does the information make the report more persuasive?

The summary section is also where diagnoses are formally stated, if appropriate. If the referral question centered around the presence or absence of a particular diagnosis, a direct answer to that question should appear in the summary. If formal diagnosis was not a central component of the referral question, the psychologist need not address the issue unless (a) the results of the testing strongly support the notion that the client's problems fit into a particular diagnostic category, and (b) stating such might be helpful to the client or the referral source.

The recommendation section should be inclusive, covering everything that would be helpful; and it should make sense to the reader. When the reasoning for a recommendation is not obvious, it should be briefly explained. For example, if there is some chance that a client's processing-speed deficits are related to problems with her vision, include a recommendation for a vision exam along with some information about why that recommendation was made: "Susie should have her vision examined to make sure that problems with visual acuity are not contributing to her slow processing speed."

Writing recommendations in narrative form is useful when there is only one recommendation, or one that is far more important than the others. In most circumstances, however, listing recommendations in order of importance makes them easier for the reader to understand. For more information about how to develop recommendations, see Chapter 7.

Results of the present evaluation indicate that John meets diagnostic criteria for ADHD of the combined type. There is no evidence of a mood disorder, but he is prone to irritability when he is required to attend to tasks after they are no longer interesting to him and when his impulses are thwarted. He expresses his emotions intensely, as is typical of children with ADHD, contributing to the sense that he is unhappy. In addition, he is frustrated with himself, and he is beginning to feel incompetent and different from his peers. These problems are secondary to ADHD and should resolve with appropriate treatment for ADHD. John's verbal and perceptual abilities are above average, but his working memory, which is related to attention and concentration, and his processing speed are both at the low end of average. This pattern of cognitive strengths and weaknesses is not unusual in children with ADHD, and it makes schoolwork challenging. He may not recall information as well as he needs to, and he works more slowly than many of his peers. These problems may improve with treatment for ADHD and also can be addressed with support and accommodations in the classroom. Finally, results indicate that John is a securely attached child who is interested in other people. With treatment for ADHD he should be able to make a good adjustment in all spheres.

Recommendations are as follows:

1. Provide treatment for ADHD, including education for John's parents. John may benefit from medical treatment, but he also would benefit from psychosocial interventions to help him learn about ADHD, including how it affects him and how he can manage it. The treatment provider should have expertise in working with young children who have ADHD and their families. [The names and contact information for providers who meet these criteria could be added here.]

2. Refer for an educational evaluation, so that John can access support and accommodations that will help him be successful at school.

(Depending on the examiner's knowledge about ADHD as well as about local resources, and also depending on whether the evaluation will be forwarded to the school or to a therapist, additional recommendations relevant to treatment and academic functioning could be added.)

CHAPTER 9

Writing Style

Psychologists conduct assessments purposefully, to understand people, solve problems, and make informed decisions. They write assessment reports to document and communicate their findings. Effective assessment reports are clear and easy to follow, accurate, and persuasive, encouraging action. The best reports are also a pleasure to read.

Clarity

Strategies for clear and effective writing in assessment reports are similar to strategies for clear and effective writing for any academic, business, or personal endeavor. Simple sentences, precise word usage, and well-organized paragraphs are the basis for well-written reports. Hart (2006) notes that "clear writing requires empathy" (p. 110); in other words, it is important for the writer to be able to appreciate how the audience will experience the report, given their level of reading ability, expertise in psychological assessment, and relationship to the client. He offers the following guidelines to improve clarity:

- Choose words familiar to the reader. Define terms that the reader might not know.

- Anticipate readers' questions.

- Provide a context that gives meaning to facts (this is the purpose of the background information section).

- Aim for readability scores that are appropriate to the reader (see below for more information about readability).

- Favor short sentences, but vary sentence length.

- Avoid common errors in grammar such as misplaced modifiers, dangling prepositions, and confusing pronouns.

William Zinsser (2001), author of the classic text *On Writing Well*, notes, "The secret of good writing is to strip every sentence to its cleanest components" (p. 7). He suggests getting rid of superfluous words and avoiding long words that are no better than short words. He also points to the importance of maintaining consistency (unity) in tense, pronouns, and mood. In *The Elements of Style*, Strunk and White (2000) advocate breaking apart overly complex sentences into two or more shorter sentences. They also recommend, in choosing words, to avoid "the elaborate, the pretentious, the coy, and the cute" (p. 76) and the use of qualifiers such as "very" and "rather."

Grammar

In making her writing clear, the writer of an assessment report faces some specific challenges related to using proper grammar. Problems in tense are particularly troublesome. Should the report be written in the present or past tense? According to Zinsser (2001), "the whole purpose of tenses is to enable a writer to deal with time in its various gradations" (p. 50) that translates to assessment reports as follows.

Report test results in the present tense: "WISC-IV results *indicate* Hannah's verbal abilities *are* in the average range . . .", "Findings from the MMPI-2 *suggest* that Joey *is* . . .", and so forth. Behavioral observations are concerned with events that took place in the past, that is, at the time of the evaluation. They are usually reported in the past tense: "John *was* cooperative . . . ", "Heather *spoke* easily about herself. . . ." Background information is reported in a mix of tenses, even though the "event" (i.e., the passing along of the information) took place in the past, at the time of the interview or the review of records: "Ms. Smith *reports* that Joey *is* a strong reader . . . ", "School records *indicate* that Tim *was expelled* from Parker High School." Interview data are discussed in the past tense: "During the interview Janey *reported* that she doesn't like . . .", "Mrs. Smith *stated* that Janey doesn't get along. . . ." Even seasoned report writers have difficulty getting the tense right. The task is made easier by reading the report aloud to hear how it sounds.

Another common problem in assessment reports, not as difficult as the problem of tense, is, as Strunk and White (2000) put it, "A participial phrase at the beginning of a sentence must refer to the grammatical subject" (p. 13). Less complicated than it sounds, this means it must be clear who or what the phrase at the beginning of a sentence is referring to. "Although he had a friend who lived nearby, *he* spent much of his time by himself" is a problem sentence because it is not clear who spent time by himself, the subject of the assessment or his friend. The easiest way to make the sentence clear is to use a name instead of a pronoun: "Although he had a friend who lived nearby, *John* spent much of his time by himself." This sentence is better, but using too many names in place of pronouns can result in awkward sentences. A better alternative is to change the sentence structure entirely without changing its meaning. "John spent much of his time by himself despite having a friend who lived nearby."

Other problems come up in assessment reports, such as ensuring that pronouns agree and that commas and semicolons are used correctly, but these kinds of writing problems are common to all sorts of writing, and they don't create special problems for the writer of assessment reports. In any case, students who lack confidence in their writing skills would benefit from getting assistance with the writing aspect of the report, making sure to protect client confidentiality. Practice helps. Although it can be a painful process, the more reports a student writes, the easier it is to write them without grammatical errors.

Wording

In addition to the general comments about the use of language, above, writers of assessment reports have special obligations to use language with precision. Poorly chosen words or sloppy sentences could result in misinterpretation of the assessment findings, an event that should be avoided at all costs. Also, it is essential to be clear about the degree of certainty in the assessment findings and their interpretation. Joan's verbal abilities are below average, she *is likely* to have trouble in school as she progresses to the higher grades (not, she *will*, because there is no way to know that for sure). Similarly, it is acceptable to speculate about the cause of a problem or what might happen in the future, but the writer needs to be clear that he is speculating about these ideas; he is not certain about them. On the other hand, too much "waffling" ("it seems that . . .", "it may . . . ") makes a report hard to read and affects the perceived credibility of the writer.

A much harder problem for report writers is avoiding the use of jargon. The assessment psychologist must communicate information about complex aspects of human functioning, so she needs to understand complex concepts well enough to explain them using everyday language. If she is going to write about them, she needs to understand and be able to explain concepts such as "reality testing," "defense mechanisms," "part-objects," and so forth. Translating jargon into everyday English is an excellent learning experience, because it requires the student to thoroughly understand extremely challenging material. It is well worth taking the time to get it right, even if it requires rereading texts or engaging in an extended discussion with a supervisor or peer.

Readability

Virginia Harvey (1997), in her article about improving readability in psychological testing reports, notes that most reports are written at a level that is far too difficult for readers, especially nonprofessionals, to comprehend. Using standard measures of readability based on Flesch and Flesch-Kincaid grade level and reading ease scores, she found that most reports prepared for a school system were in the difficult or very difficult range (mean Flesch grade levels were above 15.00). Specific training for graduate students helped lower readability levels, although the mean level remained above 13.00 even with training. She went on to make six specific suggestions to keep readability at more appropriate levels for both nonprofessional and professional audiences, as follows:

- Shorten sentence lengths
- Minimize the number of difficult words
- Reduce the use of jargon

- Reduce the use of acronyms
- Omit passive verbs
- Increase the use of subheadings (p. 274)

Accuracy

Inaccuracies can easily creep into the psychological assessment report at several junctures. In some cases, they cause harm by making the writer look bad and thus lose his credibility, so the reader has less confidence in the report's content. The reader thinks, "If the writer got the spelling of a name or a birth date wrong, what other mistakes might he have made?" The reader loses confidence in the report findings to a greater or lesser extent. In other instances, errors in the report cause harm by misleading the reader who doesn't recognize them as errors or by contributing to conclusions and recommendations that do not serve the client well. They could lead to a misdiagnosis, failure to gain admittance into a program or to access needed accommodations, a miscalculation of risk, or inadequate treatment. We describe common report errors here, along with suggestions about how to avoid making them.

Test Administration

There are all kinds of opportunities for making errors while administering tests, especially those with complex instructions. These include some cognitive, memory, and neuropsychological tests and, notably, the Rorschach. Usually, errors in test administration are easily caught prior to writing a report—most often, partway through the test. The examiner might realize that he forgot to administer a portion of the test, he gave the instructions incorrectly, or he made a mistake in timing. The examiner has to decide if the error is small enough to overlook. We recommend a conservative approach in answering this question: If you are not sure of the validity of the results, don't use the data, or report it with a full explanation of the abnormalities in test administration and a guess as to how that abnormality might have influenced the data. Another rare but not unheard of problem is cheating. The subject might be able to see the answer in the administration book. This is easily avoided but only if the examiner is aware of the possibility. Also, test subjects sometimes neglect to complete all pages of a self-report test or leave too many items out. The examiner should review the test protocol before ending the session. In the busyness of the moment, a distracted examiner might forget this minor task and be left with test protocols that are not interpretable.

The main casualty of all these errors is that less reliable data are available to the examiner than would be otherwise. These things happen. However, the likelihood of making errors during test administration can be minimized by following a few simple rules:

- Know the test well. Read the manual, especially the instructions for administering the test.

- Pay attention while administering tests, not always easy when the process is tedious.

- Use props such as a "do not forget" list and a stopwatch (instead of a second hand on a watch).

- Develop good testing habits, such as routinely noting start times and behavioral observations.

Interview and Record Review

Examiners make errors during the interview phase of an assessment when they neglect to take careful notes, thinking that they will remember what the client or informant said. They might remember, but they might not, and careful notes are a vital backup. Notes are also an important means of documenting the experience, should anyone ever question what happened. Another source of errors is taking information gained in interview and record reviews at face value, assuming too readily that the information is correct as it stands. The clients or informants can be misleading in the information they provide, often inadvertently but sometimes on purpose. They may have good reason not to disclose certain information. Although the details might not be important to the conclusion of the report, the report could be misleading to the reader and, if the reader has the correct information and the writer doesn't, the writer looks foolish and the report will not be taken as seriously as it should. A third source of errors is failing to get enough information by not asking enough questions. The examiner might forget to ask a question or might not think about asking it. For example, if the examiner asks a child about who he lives with and forgets to ask about siblings who reside elsewhere, he might not hear that a sibling is in residential treatment, lives with a grandmother, or attends Harvard. If the report doesn't mention significant background details the reader is familiar with, it loses credibility. In addition, the examiner does not have the full picture when drawing conclusions and making recommendations.

To avoid errors that arise out of the interview and record review, we recommend the following steps:

- Careful preparation, especially for new clinicians. Prepare an interview guide, a list of questions you want to know the answers to. Practice interviews via role-play. Have a friend play a reticent client and practice asking questions or otherwise encouraging him to provide the necessary information.

- Taking copious notes in every assessment situation, including notes about one's observations. Don't count on being able to remember without them.

- When writing the report, note the source of information. "School records indicate that . . .", "Ms. Smith reports that. . . . " This is also a way of noting the degree of certainty about the information. An alternative is to note the source of information at the top of the section with a statement about its presumed reliability. "The information below comes from an interview with Jane Smith, John's mother, and is thought to be reliable."

Scoring and Interpretation

Scoring test protocols, whether by hand or computer, also provides ample opportunity for errors. Scoring items or inputting data incorrectly are obvious problems, but calculation errors are also a concern. Small errors can make a significant difference in the overall score. An easy but tedious solution is to score protocols twice. If you are uncertain about how to score an item, do not be embarrassed about consulting with a supervisor or colleague. It is not unusual, even among experienced clinicians.

Errors in test interpretation or, at a broader level, in integrating data to draw conclusions, are obviously a cause for concern. A new clinician might falsely recall that a certain MMPI-2 code means something that it actually doesn't, for example. Making these errors is not a problem, but putting them into a report is.

New clinicians must remain humble. They need to look things up unless they have them, for certain, committed to memory. Most important, they need to make good use of supervision to ensure that their interpretations of test data are accurate and that they are integrating the data appropriately and drawing sensible conclusions from it. These are skills that develop with knowledge and experience.

Reporting

Some psychologists use templates when writing reports, especially when they perform routine assessments that involve a standard battery of tests and a standard report format. Forgetting to change a name, especially one buried deep into the report, is a common error. Neglecting to change pronouns throughout the report is another. Psychologists are also prone to making mistakes when listing numbers to document test scores, especially when there are a lot of scores to report. These errors can be significant because they are confusing for the reader, even if they don't affect the interpretation of data or conclusions drawn from it. To minimize errors in the written report, proofreading is essential. In addition, when listing test scores in a document, recheck the list to make sure the numbers are correct and in the right place.

Persuasiveness

According to Herbert W. Simons (2001), "Persuasion is human communication designed to influence the autonomous judgments and actions of others" (p. 7). Why should assessment reports be persuasive? Is it not enough to give tests, record results, and report the findings? Persuasion is an important goal of assessment reports, especially those that are administrative in focus, influencing decision making and access to services or special treatment. This is evident in the case of Wilma, a young woman who was diagnosed with a psychotic disorder and asked to leave her job with the police force. Wilma did not agree with the findings of the department's psychiatrist. She felt that he misinterpreted her behavior and requested a psychological evaluation for a second opinion. The job of the psychologist performing the second assessment was to persuade authorities that the first evaluation was incorrect, if he felt that the data he collected supported such a conclusion. It is also evident in the case of Jennifer, who was about to be placed in a juvenile training center (reform school). A second psychological evaluation was requested because her attorney felt that she had mental health issues that were not adequately detailed in the first report. The attorney wanted her placed in a treatment facility instead of the training school. Persuasion is important in less obvious ways too. Justin was referred for evaluation to determine his eligibility for special education services. The team deciding on whether to find him eligible had to be "persuaded"—in this case, by test scores—that he was eligible for these services. John's physician and parents were persuaded that he needed treatment for attention-deficit/hyperactivity disorder (ADHD) but not depression.

There is an element of persuasion in every psychological assessment case in which there is a problem to be solved or a decision to be made. In addition to being a record of consultation and a technical document, the assessment report can be conceived of as a "call to action." It says, "This is what's wrong and here's how to fix it," or "This individual should be accepted into the program and here's why."

According to the *American Heritage Dictionary* (2006), *rhetoric* is "the art or study of using language effectively and persuasively." There is a very extensive body of work on rhetoric in speech and writing that goes well beyond the scope of this text. Suffice it to say that what makes writing persuasive, to start, is good grammar, correct spelling, neatness, accuracy, and professionalism. These basics contribute to credibility, and credibility contributes to persuasiveness. Persuasive writing is also logical; it builds a case in an organized manner, detail by detail. By the end of the report, the conclusion should be obvious and the reader convinced of its merit.

There is also an extensive literature on persuasive communication from the field of social psychology. Interestingly, this literature has not been applied to persuasiveness in psychological assessment reports. Nevertheless, there are lessons that can readily be applied. From the social psychology literature on persuasive communication, for example, a recent article (De Wit, Das, & Vet, 2008) discusses two kinds of evidence that can be used in persuasive communications: statistical or anecdotal (facts or stories). Facts are more effective when they are consistent with the views of the receiver. Stories are better when the message is not preferred by the receiver; that is, when the message is something the receiver might not want to hear. Also, the persuasive effect of facts depends on active cognitive processing by the receiver, and receivers are most likely to consider message content when they are highly involved in an issue. A message that is inconsistent with a receiver's beliefs may heighten defensiveness. In such situations, facts have a limited affect and narrative evidence may result in less defensive responding, perhaps through its influence on "implicit, impulsive responding" rather than reflective reasoning. In other words, assessment reports that include both facts (test scores and the like) and stories (background information) may be optimal for persuasion, meeting the needs of all kinds of receivers.

In another research line, peripheral cues (vs. argument) are studied as an aspect of persuasive communication. Simple and brief cues (such as credentials of the evaluator, a long list of administered tests, or professional stationery) are thought to be especially powerful in situations in which receivers have low levels of motivation and limited capacity to follow arguments (Pierro, Mannetti, Kruglanski, & Sleeth-Keppler, 2004).

In a third research line, the influence of affect on persuasion is considered (Albarracín & Kumkale, 2003). For example, background music might result in positive attitudes and increased persuasiveness of a message. The authors note that "people develop attitudes in line with the message to a greater extent when they experience positive affect than when they experience negative affect" (p. 465). They use affect as information when they are poorly motivated or their capacity to think about the issues is limited. How could this notion apply to assessment report writing? Adding information that increases positive affect, such as hopefulness, might sway poorly motivated readers to follow recommendations. For example, noting that a certain type of treatment or approach helps many students with condition X be successful may increase optimism and promote compliance, in comparison with making a recommendation without the additional affect-related information.

This brief review of the persuasive communication literature underscores how important it is to know one's audience. If the audience is expected to have low motivation or low capacity for following arguments, or a high degree of defensiveness, an increased use of narrative evidence and positive peripheral cues might contribute to the persuasiveness of the report. Using facts to make strong arguments is effective with audiences who are motivated and have a good ability to follow the arguments. Also, the literature underscores how important it is to think about one's task, the focus of the assessment. If the goal of the report is to persuade a reluctant party to change something important, such as convincing a school program to provide services to a student that were previously denied, it is well worth paying attention to how to improve its persuasive powers.

Making Your Writing a Pleasure to Read and Finding Your Voice

Writing that is pleasurable to read flows easily. The points it makes build on each other in a seamless fashion. The reader does not have to go back and forth in the text to make sense of it. The sentence structures are easy to follow, but they have a good rhythm (Hart, 2006) and are varied, so the writing keeps the reader interested. It is also targeted at the level of the reader, so that she doesn't have to struggle to understand it. As Zinsser (2001) notes, "Good writing has an aliveness that keeps the reader reading from one paragraph to the next. . . . It's a question of using the English language in a way that will achieve the greatest clarity and strength" (pp. 5–6).

Fortunately, the goal of making reports pleasing to read is much more achievable than the goal of, for example, writing a laudable essay. It requires taking the time to smooth out sentences by improving their rhythm and structure, and taking the time to smooth out paragraphs and sections of the report by making sure they are well organized. This fine-tuning can be done after a first draft of the report is completed or as it is progressing. It can be helpful to read the report aloud to hear how it sounds. It can also be helpful to put the report away for a day or more and come back to it, to get a new perspective. Finally, getting feedback from a supervisor or a peer (taking care to protect the client's confidentiality), specifically about writing, can help a new clinician prepare material in a manner that the reader will appreciate.

Assessment reports do not have to conform to one "best practice" model, although they should meet the standards that have been outlined in this text. *Voice*, as defined by Jack Hart (2006), is "the writer's personal style coming through in the writing" (p. 195). He notes that a distinctive voice develops as the writer becomes confident and relaxed. It might arise out of a favored vocabulary, sentence structure, or pace. A personal voice prevents writing from becoming dull and formulaic. Although formulaic reports may meet basic requirements, they are likely to be uninteresting to read and boring to write. As Hart notes, "Writers who learn a workable process and a set of practical skills can create low-anxiety prose that's full of rhythm and color, rich in humanity, and high in impact" (p. 261).

Psychologists write assessment reports to solve problems and make decisions in the real world. They do this work to make a living. They need to work efficiently so they can complete their assessments on time and in a cost-effective manner. The report must be "writeable," its demands manageable for the psychologist. To be efficient, it is helpful to plan a format for the report and use it as an organizational structure. Then fill in the blanks, paragraph by paragraph. By the time the first draft of the body of the report is finished, the summary and recommendations almost write themselves. The final draft is complete after proofreading and fine-tuning the writing. There are no shortcuts, but the process is straightforward and, with practice, can be completed proficiently.

CHAPTER 10

Ethics of Assessment and Report Writing

A s psychologists apply their assessment skills in various clinical settings, ethically sound practice should remain a top priority. For this reason, we devote this chapter to the ethical practice of real-world psychological assessment. To guide our discussion, we turn to the Code of Ethics of the American Psychological Association (APA, 2002). Many of these standards relate to assessment activities. Some, including those in the sections on Competence (Section 2) and Privacy and Confidentiality (Section 4), apply to all aspects of clinical work, while those in the Assessment section (Section 9) target assessment activities specifically. In this chapter, we explore all these standards in the context of real-world clinical assessment activities. Box 10.1 presents the full text of the ethical standards most relevant to assessment.

••• Box 10.1 •••••••••••••••••••••••••••••••

APA ethical standards related to assessment

2. COMPETENCE

2.01 Boundaries of Competence

(a) Psychologists provide services, teach, and conduct research with populations and in areas only within the boundaries of their competence, based on their education, training, supervised experience, consultation, study, or professional experience.

(b) Where scientific or professional knowledge in the discipline of psychology establishes that an understanding of factors associated with age, gender, gender identity, race, ethnicity, culture, national origin, religion, sexual orientation, disability, language, or socioeconomic status is essential for effective implementation of their services or research, psychologists have or obtain the training, experience, consultation, or supervision necessary to ensure the competence of their services, or they make appropriate referrals, except as provided in Standard 2.02, Providing Services in Emergencies.

(Continued)

(Continued)

(c) Psychologists planning to provide services, teach, or conduct research involving populations, areas, techniques, or technologies new to them undertake relevant education, training, supervised experience, consultation, or study.

2.03 Maintaining Competence

Psychologists undertake ongoing efforts to develop and maintain their competence.

4. PRIVACY AND CONFIDENTIALITY

4.01 Maintaining Confidentiality

Psychologists have a primary obligation and take reasonable precautions to protect confidential information obtained through or stored in any medium, recognizing that the extent and limits of confidentiality may be regulated by law or established by institutional rules or professional or scientific relationship. (See also Standard 2.05, Delegation of Work to Others.)

4.02 Discussing the Limits of Confidentiality

(a) Psychologists discuss with persons (including, to the extent feasible, persons who are legally incapable of giving informed consent and their legal representatives) and organizations with whom they establish a scientific or professional relationship (1) the relevant limits of confidentiality and (2) the foreseeable uses of the information generated through their psychological activities. (See also Standard 3.10, Informed Consent.)

(b) Unless it is not feasible or is contraindicated, the discussion of confidentiality occurs at the outset of the relationship and thereafter as new circumstances may warrant.

(c) Psychologists who offer services, products, or information via electronic transmission inform clients/patients of the risks to privacy and limits of confidentiality.

4.03 Recording

Before recording the voices or images of individuals to whom they provide services, psychologists obtain permission from all such persons or their legal representatives. (See also Standards 8.03, Informed Consent for Recording Voices and Images in Research; 8.05, Dispensing With Informed Consent for Research; and 8.07, Deception in Research.)

4.04 Minimizing Intrusions on Privacy

(a) Psychologists include in written and oral reports and consultations, only information germane to the purpose for which the communication is made.

(b) Psychologists discuss confidential information obtained in their work only for appropriate scientific or professional purposes and only with persons clearly concerned with such matters.

9. *ASSESSMENT*

9.01 Bases for Assessments

(a) Psychologists base the opinions contained in their recommendations, reports, and diagnostic or evaluative statements, including forensic testimony, on information and techniques sufficient to substantiate their findings. (See also Standard 2.04, Bases for Scientific and Professional Judgments.)

(b) Except as noted in 9.01c, psychologists provide opinions of the psychological characteristics of individuals only after they have conducted an examination of the individuals adequate to support their statements or conclusions. When, despite reasonable efforts, such an examination is not practical, psychologists document the efforts they made and the result of those efforts, clarify the probable impact of their limited information on the reliability and validity of their opinions, and appropriately limit the nature and extent of their conclusions or recommendations. (See also Standards 2.01, Boundaries of Competence, and 9.06, Interpreting Assessment Results.)

(c) When psychologists conduct a record review or provide consultation or supervision and an individual examination is not warranted or necessary for the opinion, psychologists explain this and the sources of information on which they based their conclusions and recommendations.

9.02 Use of Assessments

(a) Psychologists administer, adapt, score, interpret, or use assessment techniques, interviews, tests, or instruments in a manner and for purposes that are appropriate in light of the research on or evidence of the usefulness and proper application of the techniques.

(b) Psychologists use assessment instruments whose validity and reliability have been established for use with members of the population tested. When such validity or reliability has not been established, psychologists describe the strengths and limitations of test results and interpretation.

(c) Psychologists use assessment methods that are appropriate to an individual's language preference and competence, unless the use of an alternative language is relevant to the assessment issues.

9.03 Informed Consent in Assessments

(a) Psychologists obtain informed consent for assessments, evaluations, or diagnostic services, as described in Standard 3.10, Informed Consent, except when (1) testing is mandated by law or governmental regulations; (2) informed consent is implied because testing is conducted as a routine educational, institutional, or organizational activity (e.g., when participants voluntarily agree to assessment when applying for a job); or (3) one purpose of the testing is to evaluate decisional capacity. Informed consent includes an explanation of the nature and purpose of the assessment, fees, involvement of third parties, and limits of confidentiality and sufficient opportunity for the client/patient to ask questions and receive answers.

(b) Psychologists inform persons with questionable capacity to consent or for whom testing is mandated by law or governmental regulations about the nature and purpose of the proposed assessment services, using language that is reasonably understandable to the person being assessed.

(Continued)

(Continued)

(c) Psychologists using the services of an interpreter obtain informed consent from the client/patient to use that interpreter, ensure that confidentiality of test results and test security are maintained, and include in their recommendations, reports, and diagnostic or evaluative statements, including forensic testimony, discussion of any limitations on the data obtained. (See also Standards 2.05, Delegation of Work to Others; 4.01, Maintaining Confidentiality; 9.01, Bases for Assessments; 9.06, Interpreting Assessment Results; and 9.07, Assessment by Unqualified Persons.)

9.04 Release of Test Data

(a) The term *test data* refers to raw and scaled scores, client/patient responses to test questions or stimuli, and psychologists' notes and recordings concerning client/patient statements and behavior during an examination. Those portions of test materials that include client/patient responses are included in the definition of *test data.* Pursuant to a client/patient release, psychologists provide test data to the client/patient or other persons identified in the release. Psychologists may refrain from releasing test data to protect a client/patient or others from substantial harm or misuse or misrepresentation of the data or the test, recognizing that in many instances release of confidential information under these circumstances is regulated by law. (See also Standard 9.11, Maintaining Test Security.)

(b) In the absence of a client/patient release, psychologists provide test data only as required by law or court order.

9.05 Test Construction

Psychologists who develop tests and other assessment techniques use appropriate psychometric procedures and current scientific or professional knowledge for test design, standardization, validation, reduction or elimination of bias, and recommendations for use.

9.06 Interpreting Assessment Results

When interpreting assessment results, including automated interpretations, psychologists take into account the purpose of the assessment as well as the various test factors, test-taking abilities, and other characteristics of the person being assessed, such as situational, personal, linguistic, and cultural differences, that might affect psychologists' judgments or reduce the accuracy of their interpretations. They indicate any significant limitations of their interpretations. (See also Standards 2.01b and c, Boundaries of Competence, and 3.01, Unfair Discrimination.)

9.07 Assessment by Unqualified Persons

Psychologists do not promote the use of psychological assessment techniques by unqualified persons, except when such use is conducted for training purposes with appropriate supervision. (See also Standard 2.05, Delegation of Work to Others.)

9.08 Obsolete Tests and Outdated Test Results

(a) Psychologists do not base their assessment or intervention decisions or recommendations on data or test results that are outdated for the current purpose.

(b) Psychologists do not base such decisions or recommendations on tests and measures that are obsolete and not useful for the current purpose.

9.09 Test Scoring and Interpretation Services

(a) Psychologists who offer assessment or scoring services to other professionals accurately describe the purpose, norms, validity, reliability, and applications of the procedures and any special qualifications applicable to their use.

(b) Psychologists select scoring and interpretation services (including automated services) on the basis of evidence of the validity of the program and procedures as well as on other appropriate considerations. (See also Standard 2.01b and c, Boundaries of Competence.)

(c) Psychologists retain responsibility for the appropriate application, interpretation, and use of assessment instruments, whether they score and interpret such tests themselves or use automated or other services.

9.10 Explaining Assessment Results

Regardless of whether the scoring and interpretation are done by psychologists, by employees or assistants, or by automated or other outside services, psychologists take reasonable steps to ensure that explanations of results are given to the individual or designated representative unless the nature of the relationship precludes provision of an explanation of results (such as in some organizational consulting, preemployment or security screenings, and forensic evaluations), and this fact has been clearly explained to the person being assessed in advance.

9.11. Maintaining Test Security

The term *test materials* refers to manuals, instruments, protocols, and test questions or stimuli and does not include *test data* as defined in Standard 9.04, Release of Test Data. Psychologists make reasonable efforts to maintain the integrity and security of test materials and other assessment techniques consistent with law and contractual obligations, and in a manner that permits adherence to this Ethics Code.

SOURCE: APA (2002).

Competence in Assessment

Perhaps it sounds obvious that psychologists conducting assessments should be competent, but the principle of competence as applied to assessment is nonetheless essential. In particular, psychologists must recognize their own specific competencies when they engage in assessment. General qualifications such as possessing a doctoral degree, completing assessment courses, or being licensed do not automatically make a psychologist competent to conduct any particular assessment. Instead, competence is determined by the match between the activities demanded by the particular assessment task and the specific abilities of the psychologist conducting that assessment (Knapp & VandeCreek, 2006). Or, as stated in Ethical Standard 2.01(a), psychologists should practice assessment "only within the boundaries of their competence, based on their education, training, supervised experience, consultation, study, or professional experience" (APA, 2002, p. 1063).

The rationale for basing competence on specific skills rather than general qualifications seems strong when we consider the broad range of assessment techniques that psychologists, as a professional group, might conduct. Hundreds, if not thousands, of specific tests are available to psychologists interested in assessing intelligence, achievement, personality variables, behavior patterns, neuropsychological issues, depression, anxiety, and many other domains. In a practical sense, it is simply beyond the abilities of any individual psychologist to be competent in all techniques. As an example, consider Dr. Hildago, a licensed psychologist, whose primary professional activity involves intellectual assessment of adult clients. Dr. Hildago's graduate training included courses and supervision in adult assessment, and she has obtained additional training in adult assessment since earning her doctoral degree. Dr. Hildago has significant expertise in the current edition of the Wechsler Adult Intelligence Scale (WAIS). Despite her expertise, training, and experience, if Dr. Hildago receives a request to assess the IQ of a 4-year-old child, she should recognize that she is unqualified to conduct the assessment unless she obtains additional training and supervision, specifically in the use of a test such as the Wechsler Preschool and Primary Scale of Intelligence (WPPSI). The specific training or supervision needed to qualify a psychologist to administer, score, and interpret a particular test can be difficult to pinpoint but efforts to offer some guidance have been made (e.g., Turner, DeMers, Fox, & Reed, 2001). Psychologists who fail to recognize the boundaries of their competence, or who believe that they are somehow competent across the board, pose a danger to the clients they serve, and ultimately to their own careers, when they overextend themselves as assessors.

The example above, involving Dr. Hildago, involved client age, but age is not the only client variable that psychologists must consider when they make efforts to ensure their competence in assessment. Standard 2.01(b) states that psychologists' competence depends on their understanding of clients' "age, gender, gender identity, race, ethnicity, culture, national origin, religion, sexual orientation, disability, language, or socioeconomic status" (APA, 2002, p. 1064). So when conducting assessments, ethical psychologists make sure that their approach to clients incorporates an appreciation of a wide range of client variables. As an example, consider Maria, a Cuban immigrant, referred to Dr. Stevens for an assessment as a result of recent depressive behavior. Without an appreciation of Maria's ethnicity, culture, and language, not to mention other variables that may be relevant, various aspects of Dr. Stevens's assessment, including the selection of techniques, the interpretation of results, and suggestions for improvement, could be misguided.

In addition to stating that psychologists must *obtain* competence, the APA code of ethics also states that psychologists must *maintain* competence. Standard 2.03 states that psychologists "undertake ongoing efforts to develop and maintain their competence" (APA, 2002, p. 1064). This standard is consistent with the laws of many states requiring continuing education of psychologists. With regard to assessment, psychologists should remain abreast of changes in the field, such as new editions of tests and emerging data on the reliability and validity of various techniques.

Confidentiality in Assessment

Like competence, confidentiality is a broad ethical principle with many important applications in the practice of assessment. Generally, psychologists conducting assessments must "protect confidential information obtained through or stored in any medium" (Standard 4.01; APA, 2002, p. 1066). This includes not only information collected from clients in traditional, face-to-face settings, such as interviews and testing, but also information collected over the phone, via e-mail, or by other electronic means. Thus, psychologists should ensure that their phone conversations are entirely private, and their electronic interactions can't be intercepted by prying eyes. The conveniences provided by technology can provide confidentiality concerns for psychologists; for example, sending or receiving faxes on shared fax machines or leaving voice-mail messages that can be heard by more than one individual, such as on a client's home answering machine, can be problematic (e.g., Fisher, 2003). Careful forethought about these issues is a must for the psychologist. Often, discussing these issues with clients or others involved in assessments, prior to taking any action, can prevent ethical problems from taking place. For instance, a psychologist who clarifies up front with an assessment client where phone messages can be left—for example, cell phone, work phone, home phone—can avoid an unintentional breach of confidentiality.

Another discussion that should take place early in the relationship between the assessor and the client involves the limits of confidentiality. Ethical Standard 4.02(a) states that psychologists should discuss with clients "the relevant limits of confidentiality" and "the foreseeable uses of the information generated through their psychological activities" (APA, 2002, p. 1066). This discussion typically happens at the outset of the relationship (per Standard 4.02[b]), and it should include a discussion or electronically transmitted communications, when relevant (per Standard 4.02[c]). The importance of discussing the limits of confidentiality is emphasized by the finding that most individuals outside of the mental health profession assume that there are no such limits and that psychologist-client confidentiality is absolute (Miller & Thelen, 1986). Thus, to clarify any misconceptions held by assessment clients, discussions of the limits of confidentiality are essential.

What exactly are the limits of confidentiality regarding information obtained during an assessment? The answer to this question can depend on specifics of a clinical situation and on laws or regulations, often related to child abuse, that vary from state to state, but the "duty to warn" established by the *Tarasoff* court case looms large. The essential facts of the *Tarasoff* case are relatively straightforward. In 1969, a college student told his psychologist at his university's counseling center that he intended to kill his girlfriend. The psychologist took the client's comment seriously and contacted campus police about the matter. The campus police officers interviewed the student but released him. Tragically, the student did kill his girlfriend, whose name was Tatiana Tarasoff. Following her death, the victim's family filed a suit, and the court found that the psychologist was in fact liable for failing to warn Tarasoff of the danger. This finding set a precedent for mental health professionals whereby they must balance their obligation to keep clinical information confidential with their duty to warn potential victims of danger—a very difficult challenge indeed (Knapp & VandeCreek, 2006).

Although the *Tarasoff* case took place in the context of psychotherapy, similar situations could undoubtedly arise in the context of assessment. In other words, while conducting interviews or psychological tests, psychologists could receive information from clients regarding their intent to inflict harm. However, psychologists in these situations must consider numerous questions, none of which have easy answers. How credible is the client? How should the psychologist determine this credibility? How identifiable is the potential victim? What constitutes sufficient danger to break confidentiality and warn a potential victim—life-and-death situations only or less severe threats as well? As an example, consider an assessment in which Dr. Yu is interviewing Max, a 39-year-old client, who works for a large corporation. Max was referred for an evaluation as a result of dramatic mood swings and erratic behavior over the past few months. During the course of the interview, Max states that he "hates some of the people" at his company who he perceives as "taunting" him and that "sometimes, I imagine giving them exactly what they deserve." Does Max's statement warrant a breach of confidentiality and warning by Dr. Yu? If so, to whom should he direct his warning? Is Dr. Yu obligated to seek more information from Max about the identities of potential victims? How should Dr. Yu determine the credibility of Max's statement? Should he take into consideration Max's history of violent behavior or lack thereof? If Dr. Yu does break confidentiality to warn potential victims, what effect will that decision have on his ability to continue the assessment with Max? Such questions are complex for psychologists conducting assessments, but as Standard 4.02 indicates, ethical psychologists communicate to their assessment clients that, although they are committed to holding client information confidential, there are limits to that confidentiality.

Standard 4.03 discusses the use of recording devices such as audio or video recorders, which some psychologists find useful during the process of assessment. According to the ethical standard, psychologists must obtain permission from clients before recording their voices or images. There are certainly benefits to the psychologist who records assessment sessions. For example, even the best note taker can't jot down all relevant information from an interview and might be distracted while attempting to do so. And for some tests that involve writing down the client's verbal responses (e.g., Wechsler intelligence tests, projective tests such as the Rorschach or Thematic Apperception Test [TAT]), a recording of the client's words can prove helpful in verifying responses. However, assessors should also consider potential drawbacks to recording, such as client self-consciousness and a decrease in willingness to disclose information. For this reason, in addition to giving clients the option to decline recording, psychologists would also be wise to explain to their clients how the recording will enhance their ability to conduct the assessment. Such information might increase a client's willingness to allow recording to take place during an assessment session.

In addition to the confidentiality of the information gathered from clients and others during an assessment, the confidentiality of the report written by the psychologist is of paramount concern. Standard 4.04(a) addresses one aspect of this confidentiality by stating that "psychologists include in written and oral reports and consultations only information germane to the purpose for which the communication is made" (APA, 2002, p. 1066). In other words, the psychologists' report should not contain information irrelevant to the referral question that initiated the assessment. As an example, consider Clara, a 9-year-old third grader, referred by her teachers to Dr. Silver for a learning disability assessment. During the initial interview, Clara reveals detailed information about the serious financial problems her parents are experiencing. She has learned this information by overhearing discussions and arguments between her parents. Dr. Silver did not ask about these issues but Clara brought them up nonetheless. In his report to Clara's teachers, Dr. Silver should include information directly related to the learning disability question, such as data from intelligence and achievement tests, but should not include the details Clara shared about her parents' financial problems. If these problems are causing Clara anxiety, and this anxiety affects her performance at school or during the assessment, Dr. Silver may choose to mention anxiety as a general factor influencing Clara's performance, but including details about her parent's finances is beyond the scope of necessary information for Clara's teachers.

Obtaining Informed Consent to Assessment

In the previous section, we discussed the importance of informing clients at the outset of an assessment about the limits of confidentiality. Actually, the limits of confidentiality are only one of a range of topics about which clients should be informed before they consent to the assessment process. As stated in Ethical Standard 9.03(a), informed consent "includes an explanation of the nature and purpose of the assessment, fees, involvement of third parties, and limits of confidentiality and sufficient opportunity for the client/patient to ask questions and receive answers" (APA, 2002, p. 1071). The rationale behind the requirement to obtain informed consent centers on clients' rights to understand the assessment process before agreeing to participate in it.

The "explanation of the nature and purpose of the assessment," as described in the ethical standard, could take many forms. Some psychologists may believe that the assessment is straightforward and simple enough and that a brief explanation may suffice; others may believe that the assessment is complex enough to warrant a much longer explanation. Similarly, the "involvement of third parties" could involve a brief summary of the parties involved or a detailed description of the roles and rights of each, and as discussed earlier, the "limits of confidentiality" is a topic about which there is little consensus. Therefore, the insistence in the ethical code to provide "sufficient opportunity for the client/patient to ask questions and receive answers" is a vital part of the informed consent process. Regardless of the attention that the psychologist devotes to informing the client, including the use of written documents, the client may remain unclear about any number of components of the assessment. Ethically, the psychologist should not proceed with the assessment until the client has had the chance to ask all such questions, and the psychologist has sufficiently addressed them.

The informed consent process should begin at the outset of the assessment, but it need not end there. Indeed, there may be some information, including answers to some client questions, that the psychologist can't answer adequately at the beginning of the first session. Numerous scholars on the topic of informed consent in psychology have supported the "process" model over the "event" model of informed consent, suggesting that informed consent is not a onetime event but an ongoing process (e.g., Berg, Appelbaum, Lidz, & Parker, 2001; O'Neill, 1998; Pomerantz, 2005). These books and articles focus primarily on psychotherapy, but it is reasonable to extend their conclusions to assessment as well, at least to some extent. As an example, consider a client referred for a court-ordered full psychological evaluation involving intellectual, neuropsychological, and personality testing. If the client walks into the first meeting with the psychologist and asks how long it will be until the assessment is complete, the psychologist may not be able to offer a definitive answer. At that early point in the assessment process, there are many things the psychologist does not yet know: how quickly the client will complete various tests; how much or how little the client will speak during interviews, which could drastically alter their length; how long it will take the psychologist to contact any third parties providing information about the client; how well the client's and psychologist's schedules match in terms of scheduling additional appointments; and whether additional tests may be deemed necessary based on the results of the tests administered initially. Rather than manufacturing a guess, it might be more appropriate for the psychologist to tell the client that a more definitive answer to that question can be provided only after a few sessions.

Regarding the questions that clients may ask, Pomerantz and Handelsman (2004) created a list of questions that psychologists might choose to provide to clients to facilitate the informed consent process. This list focuses on clients seeking psychotherapy, but an adaptation of this list may facilitate the assessment-informed consent process as well. The list includes dozens of questions on a wide variety of topics, including the nature and purpose of the meetings, duration, scheduling, confidentiality, fees, and involvement of managed care and other third parties. By giving clients the opportunity to ask as many or as few questions as they choose, psychologists satisfy that component of the ethical standard.

Since assessments often involve numerous individuals beyond the client, it can be helpful to inform all parties of the "ground rules" of the assessment early in the process. Even if the client is the only party from whom informed consent is formally required, the psychologist can prevent misunderstandings and misguided expectations by providing accurate information to all parties involved in an assessment. For example, if an employer refers an employee for an evaluation, the employer may assume that she will automatically receive a copy of the psychologists' report. In some arrangements—for example, if the employee seeks and pays for the evaluation independently—this may be a mistaken assumption. Clarifying this with the employer at the outset may save all parties the frustration when the assessment is complete.

Selecting Assessment Techniques

Assuming that the client has provided the informed consent, the assessment goes forth. But as we have learned throughout this book, assessments can differ drastically from one another, even when the referral questions are similar. The selection of particular assessment techniques is crucial not only to the assessor's ability to answer the referral question but also to the ethicality of the assessment.

Ethical Standard 9.02(a) states that psychologists select and use assessment techniques "in a manner and for purposes that are appropriate in light of the research on or evidence of the usefulness and proper application of the techniques" (APA, 2002, p. 1071). That is, psychologists should use tests only as they are intended to be used and supported by research (Adams & Luscher, 2003). Test manuals typically begin with clear descriptions of the purpose of the test and often contain substantial research supporting their use for that purpose. Psychologists should use these manuals and additional published research on the tests they cover to guide their decisions about the appropriate use of particular tests.

In addition to tests being used for appropriate purposes, they should also be used with appropriate clients. As stated in Standard 9.02(b), psychologists should use tests "whose validity and reliability have been established for use with members of the population tested" (APA, 2002, p. 1071). Typically, a test's manual will specify the population on which its norms were established, including the age range, gender, and other descriptors of the population; sometimes, such information comes from research published after the test and its manual were released. The clients with whom psychologists use that test should match the population for whom it has been deemed valid and reliable; if the client differs from that group, the psychologist should discuss the limitations of the results of the test in the report (Adams & Luscher, 2003; APA, 2002). Cultural, racial, and ethnic variables are especially relevant to this ethical standard. Some tests that have established reliability and validity with the majority group may not have such established reliability or validity with particular minority groups. Unfortunately, there are often few preferable alternatives for particular cultural groups. Where such alternatives exist, they should be selected.

Related to the question of the cultural validity of a test is its linguistic appropriateness for a particular client. Standard 9.02(c) states that psychologists should use assessment methods "appropriate to an individual's language preference and competence" unless the use of a secondary language is a component of the referral question. Some tests, including many of the most widely accepted among psychologists, such as the Wechsler intelligence tests and the Minnesota Multiphasic Personality Inventory (MMPI-2), are available in multiple languages. The rationale for offering these tests in a variety of languages is to ensure the fair and accurate assessment of clients with various linguistic fluencies. As an example, consider a psychologist assessing the IQ of a 7-year-old boy whose family had recently moved from Israel to the United States. If the boy's primary language is Hebrew, a Wechsler Intelligence Scale for Children-Fourth Edition (WISC-IV) administered in English is likely to underestimate his IQ, and the resulting report could mistakenly contribute to the boy receiving inappropriate educational services. Psychologists in this situation should diligently determine the primary language of the client and choose tests accordingly. Some tests, especially in the area of intelligence, have been developed that minimize dependence on language; thus, they may be an appropriate choice when language proves to be a significant barrier. For example, the Universal Nonverbal Intelligence Test (UNIT), published in 1996, is a language-free test of intelligence in which all the psychologists' instructions and all the client's responses involve hand gestures rather than spoken words (McCallum & Bracken, 2005).

Drawing Conclusions and Communicating Results

Once the techniques have been administered and scored, the psychologist's task is to draw conclusions and communicate the results of the assessment. Of course, as stated in Standard 9.01(a), the conclusions that psychologists reach should be based "on information and techniques sufficient to substantiate their findings" (APA, 2002, p. 1071). Psychologists' findings should neither be overly inferential nor based on unsupported or "loose" interpretations of the data collected. As an informal check on the extent to which their conclusions are substantiated, psychologists can envision themselves in a court of law defending what they have included in their assessment report. Of course, psychologists make such courtroom appearances very rarely, but imagining oneself standing up for the conclusions drawn from the assessment data can prevent the inclusion of dubious statements.

Some statements included among an assessment's conclusions are dubious because they are stated too strongly or definitively. Adams and Luscher (2003) recommend the use of qualified conclusions that do not overstate the findings of the assessment. They assert that assessment techniques rarely provide results that are unequivocal or indisputable. Therefore, the statement "This client is schizophrenic" might be overly definitive. Instead, they recommend a more tempered statement: "The results of the current assessment indicate that the client demonstrates characteristics similar to those diagnosed with schizophrenia." Of course, psychologists should not understate their findings either, but careful wording of conclusions can avoid statements that are stronger than the data supports.

When interpreting assessment data, psychologists should consider the context in which it was collected. That is, the data should not be interpreted in a vacuum. As stated in Standard 9.06, psychologists interpreting assessment data should "take into account . . . the various test factors, test-taking abilities, and other characteristics of the person being assessed, such as situational, personal, linguistic, and cultural differences" (APA, 2002, p. 1072). This standard highlights the difference between testing and assessment. Assessment goes a step beyond testing in that it incorporates the factors surrounding and possibly influencing the test results, as well as the test results themselves. A full-scale IQ score of 85 on a Wechsler intelligence scale, an elevated Scale 4 on the MMPI-2, or a high score on the Beck Depression Inventory may not mean exactly the same thing for clients taking the tests under different circumstances. The immediate context in which the client took the test, such as their physical wellness or illness, as well as cultural or linguistic factors, such as their willingness to disclose difficulties to others, can have powerful influences on their scores.

Of course, no conclusions should be drawn from outdated test results or tests that have become obsolete. Standard 9.08 asserts that psychologists should not base their assessment conclusions on "data or test results that are outdated for the current purpose" or "on tests and measures that are obsolete and not useful for the current purpose" (APA, 2002, p. 1072). On some occasions, there may be good reasons to use an older version of a test rather than the most recent update, such as a need to compare pre- and postscores after a head injury, or when research on a brand new edition is extremely limited (Knapp & VandeCreek, 2006). However, psychologists generally should avoid clinging to obsolete tests when legitimate newer editions are available, and they should replace outdated results with more recent results to serve a similar purpose. For example, consider Dr. Peterson, a psychologist, whose job routinely involves the determination of learning disabilities. When new editions of established tests such as the Wechsler tests or the Woodcock-Johnson achievement tests are published, accompanied by data to support their reliability and validity, Dr. Peterson should adopt them even if doing so requires learning the details of the new edition and abandoning the previous edition, with which he was very familiar. Additionally, if Dr. Peterson is contacted by parents of a 10th grader whose most recent learning disability testing took place when she was in 2nd grade, Dr. Peterson should insist on a new round of testing rather than agreeing to make a learning disability determination based on such outdated data.

Sometimes, psychologists have the option to pay for their clients' tests to be scored or interpreted by an automated, often computer-based, service. Such services can save the psychologist time and may seem like a cost-efficient alternative, but Standard 9.09 reminds psychologists to "select scoring and interpretation services . . . on the basis of evidence of the validity of the program and procedures" (APA, 2002, p. 1072). Moreover, psychologists "retain responsibility . . . whether they score and interpret such tests themselves or use automated or other services" (p. 1072). Thus, psychologists must not mistakenly think that they are "handing off" the scoring or interpretation of their clients' tests to others; instead, they should make decisions about automated scoring or interpretation services cautiously and with the knowledge that they remain accountable.

Regardless of the results produced by the assessment or the source of the referral question, the psychologist generally has an obligation to provide feedback to the person who has been assessed. Unless it was made clear to the client during the informed consent procedure that no results would be offered to him or her, as is the case in some forensic evaluations, some employment-related evaluations, and a few other situations, the psychologist should "take reasonable steps to ensure that explanations of results are given to the individual" according to Standard 9.10 (APA, 2002, p. 1072). Results can be communicated in a variety of ways, including providing a copy of the report or holding an in-person meeting, but regardless of the method, the psychologists' intent should be to describe the findings of the assessment in language that the client can understand, and to the extent possible, find beneficial.

Test Security Issues

When communicating assessment findings to clients or other interested parties, or when conducting any aspect of assessment, psychologists should always strive to maintain test security. In other words, they should not allow the content of psychological tests to enter the public domain. In short, test materials are the items, questions, protocols, and stimuli that constitute psychological tests, as well as the manuals that include explicit discussion of these items. According to Standard 9.11, psychologists should "make reasonable efforts to maintain the integrity and security of test materials and other assessment techniques" (APA, 2002, p. 1072). Violations of this standard could result in public awareness of the actual content of psychological tests, which could facilitate premeditated, planned, or coached responses. Such responses could, in turn, lead to fraudulent test results and undesirable real-world consequences, such as a child being mistakenly placed in the wrong educational program or a psychologically unstable adult being recommended for release from a mental institution. So psychologists must be careful not to provide explicit information about test items or questions when providing the assessment results, because once the report is out of the psychologist's office, the psychologist can no longer control its use. Especially in the age of the Internet, misuse of test materials is something about which psychologists should be vigilant (Knapp & VandeCreek, 2006).

The release of test data is an entirely different matter from the release of test materials. According to Standard 9.04, test data "refers to raw and scaled scores, client/patient responses to test questions or stimuli, and psychologists' notes and recordings concerning client/patient statements and behavior during an examination" (APA, 2002, p. 1071). In other words, unlike test materials which are generally uniform across clients, test data are the responses and other information that each client uniquely contributes to the assessment. If clients request their own test data by signing the appropriate release, "psychologists provide test data to the client/patient or other persons identified in the release" (p. 1071) unless they have reason to refuse to do so to protect someone from "substantial harm or misuse or misrepresentation of the data or the test" (p. 1072). This guidance to provide clients with their own test data represents a significant change from the previous edition of the APA ethical code (APA, 1992). In the 1992 code, psychologists were instructed to release test data only to qualified persons, and the assumption was often made that clients who lacked training in the mental health professions were unqualified. The revision of this stance in the 2002 code is consistent with the more general societal trend toward patient autonomy (Fisher, 2003; Knapp & VandeCreek, 2006).

References

Adams, H. E., & Luscher, K. A. (2003). Ethical considerations in psychological assessment. In W. O'Donohue & K. Ferguson (Eds.), *Handbook of professional ethics for psychologists: Issues, questions, and controversies* (pp. 275–283). Thousand Oaks, CA: Sage.

Albarracín, D., & Kumkale, G. T. (2003). Affect as information in persuasion: A model of affect identification and discounting. *Journal of Personality and Social Psychology, 84*(3), 453–469.

American Heritage Dictionary of the English Language (4th ed.). (2006). New York: Houghton Mifflin.

American Psychiatric Association. (2000). *Diagnostic and statistical manual of mental disorders* (4th ed., Text rev.). Washington, DC: Author.

American Psychological Association (APA). (1992). Ethical principles of psychologists and code of conduct. *American Psychologist, 47,* 1597–1611.

American Psychological Association (APA). (2002). Ethical principles of psychologists and code of conduct. *American Psychologist, 57,* 1060–1073.

Antony, M. M., & Rowa, K. (2005). Evidence-based assessment of anxiety disorders in adults. *Psychological Assessment, 17,* 256–266.

APA Presidential Task Force on Evidence-Based Practice. (2006). Evidence-based practice in psychology. *American Psychologist, 61,* 271–285.

Archer, R. P. (1997). *MMPI-A: Assessing adolescent psychopathology* (2nd ed.). Mahwah, NJ: Lawrence Erlbaum.

Baer, R. A., & Rinaldo, J. C. (2004). The Minnesota Multiphasic Personality Inventory-Adolescent (MMPI-A). In M. J. Hilsenroth & D. L. Segal (Eds.), *Comprehensive handbook of psychological assessment: Personality assessment* (Vol. 2, pp. 213–223). Hoboken, NJ: Wiley.

Barlow, D. H. (2005). What's new about evidence-based assessment? *Psychological Assessment, 17,* 308–311.

Bellak, L. (1993). *The TAT, CAT, and SAT in clinical use* (5th ed.). Boston: Allyn & Bacon.

Berg, J. W., Appelbaum, P. S., Lidz, C. W., & Parker, L. S. (2001). *Informed consent: Legal theory and clinical practice* (2nd ed.). New York: Oxford University Press.

Brody, N. (2000). History of theories and measurements of intelligence. In R. J. Sternberg (Ed.), *Handbook of intelligence* (pp. 16–33). Cambridge, UK: Cambridge University Press.

Brown, S. A., Myers, M. G., Mott, M. A., & Vik, P. W. (1994). How do teens fare after substance abuse treatment? *Applied and Preventive Psychology, 3,* 61–73.

Brown, T. E. (1996). *Brown attention-deficit disorder scales for adolescents and adults manual.* San Antonio, TX: Psychological Corporation.

Brown, T. E. (2005). *Attention deficit disorder: The unfocused mind in children and adolescents.* New Haven, CT: Yale University Press.

Butcher, J. N., & Beutler, L. E. (2003). The MMPI-2. In L. E. Beutler & G. Groth-Marnat (Eds.), *Integrative assessment of adult personality* (2nd ed., pp. 157–191). New York: Guilford Press.

Butcher, J. N., Dahlstrom, W. G., Graham, J. R., Tellegen, A., & Kaemmer, B. (1989). *Minnesota Multiphasic Personality Inventory-2: Manual for administration and scoring.* Minneapolis: University of Minnesota Press.

Butcher, J. N., Williams, C. L., Graham, J. R., Archer, R. P., Tellegen, A., Ben-Porath, Y. S., et al. (1992). *Minnesota Multiphasic Personality Inventory—Adolescent: Manual for administration, scoring, and interpretation.* Minneapolis: University of Minnesota Press.

Camara, W. J., Nathan, J. S., & Puente, A. E. (2000). Psychological test usage: Implications in professional psychology. *Professional Psychology: Research and Practice, 31*(2), 141–154.

Carroll, J. B. (2005). The three-stratum theory of cognitive abilities. In D. P. Flanagan & P. L. Harrison (Eds.), *Contemporary intellectual assessment: Theories, tests, and issues* (2nd ed., pp. 69–76). New York: Guilford Press.

Conners, C. K. (2003). *Conners' rating scales: Revised technical Manual.* North Tonawanda, NY: Multi-Health Systems.

Costa, P. T., Jr., & McCrae, R. R. (1992). *Revised NEO Personality Inventory (NEO-PI-R) and NEO Five Factor Inventory (NEO-FFI) professional manual.* Odessa, FL: Psychological Assessment Resources.

Costa, P. T., & Widiger, T. A. (Eds.). (2001). *Personality disorders and the five-factor model of personality* (2nd ed.). Washington, DC: American Psychological Association.

De Wit, J. B. F., Das, E., & Vet, R. (2008, January). What works best: Objective statistics or a personal testimonial? An assessment of the persuasive effects of different types of message evidence on risk perception. *Health Psychology, 27*(1), 110–115.

Di Nardo, P. A., & Barlow, D. H. (1988). *Anxiety Disorders Interview Schedule—Revised (ADIS R).* Albany, NY: Graywind.

Donnay, D. A. C., & Elliott, T. R. (2003). The California Psychological Inventory. In L. E. Beutler & G. Groth-Marnat (Eds.), *Integrative assessment of adult personality* (2nd ed., pp. 227–261). New York: Guilford Press.

Exner, J. E., Jr. (1986). *The Rorschach: A comprehensive system* (2nd ed.). New York: Wiley.

First, M. B., Gibbon, M., Spitzer, R. L., Williams, J. B. W., & Benjamin, L. S. (1997). *User's guide for the Structured Clinical Interview for DSM-IV Axis II personality disorders.* Washington, DC: American Psychiatric Press.

First, M. B., Spitzer, R. L., Gibbon, M., & Williams, J. B. W. (1997a). *User's guide for the Structured Clinical Interview for DSM-IV Axis I disorders: Clinician version.* Washington, DC: American Psychiatric Press.

First, M. B., Spitzer, R. L., Gibbon, M., & Williams, J. B. W. (1997b). *Structured Clinical Interview for DSM-IV Axis I disorders: Clinician version.* Washington, DC: American Psychiatric Press.

Fisher, C. B. (2003). *Decoding the ethics code: A practical guide for psychologists.* Thousand Oaks, CA: Sage.

Fletcher, J. M., Francis, D. J., Morris, R. D., & Lyon, G. R. (2005). Evidence-based assessment of learning disabilities in children and adolescents. *Journal of Clinical Child and Adolescent Psychology, 34,* 506–522.

Frauenhoffer, D., Ross, M. J., Gfeller, J., Searight, H. R., & Piotrowski, C. (1998). Psychological test usage among licensed mental health practitioners: A multidisciplinary survey. *Journal of Psychological Practice, 4,* 28–33.

Ganellen, R. J. (2007). Assessing normal and abnormal personality functioning: Strengths and weaknesses of self-report, observer, and performance-based methods. *Journal of Personality Assessment, 89*(1), 30–40.

Garb, H. N. (1998). *Studying the clinician: Judgment research and psychological assessment.* Washington, DC: American Psychological Association.

Gillberg, C., Gillberg, C., Rastam, M., & Wentz, E. (2001). The Asperger Syndrome (and high-functioning autism) Diagnostic Interview (ASDI): A preliminary study of a new structured clinical interview. *Autism, 5,* 57–66.

Greene, R. L., & Clopton, J. R. (2004). Minnesota Multiphasic Personality Inventory—2 (MMPI-2). In M. W. Maruish (Ed.), *The use of psychological testing for treatment planning and outcomes assessment* (3rd ed., Vol. 3, pp. 449–477). Mahwah, NJ: Erlbaum.

Groth-Marnat, G. (1999). *Handbook of psychological assessment* (3rd ed.). New York: Wiley.

Hart, J. (2006). *A writer's coach: The complete guide to writing strategies that work.* New York: Anchor Books.

Harvey, V. S. (1997, June). Improving readability of psychological reports. *Professional Psychology: Research and Practice, 28*(3), 271–274.

Helmes, E. (2000). Learning and memory. In G. Groth-Marnat (Ed.), *Neuropsychological assessment in clinical practice* (pp. 293–334). New York: Wiley.

Hunsley, J., & Mash, E. J. (2007). Evidence-based assessment. *Annual Review of Clinical Psychology, 3,* 29–51.

Hunsley, J., & Meyer, G. J. (2003, December). The incremental validity of psychological testing and assessment: Conceptual, methodological, and statistical issues. *Psychological Assessment, 15*(4), 446–455.

Johnston, C., & Murray, C. (2003). Incremental validity in the psychological assessment of children and adolescents. *Psychological Assessment, 15,* 496–507.

Kamphaus, R. W., & Kroncke, A. P. (2004). "Back to the future" of the Stanford-Binet Intelligence Scales. In M. Hersen (Ed.), *Comprehensive handbook of psychological assessment* (Vol. 1, pp. 77–86). New York: Wiley.

Kamphaus, R. W., Petoskey, M. D., & Rowe, E. W. (2000, April). Current trends in psychological testing of children. *Professional Psychology: Research and Practice, 31*(2), 155–164.

Klein, D. N., Dougherty, L. R., & Olino, T. M. (2005). Toward guidelines for evidence-based assessment of depression in children and adolescents. *Journal of Clinical Child and Adolescent Psychology, 34,* 412–432.

Knapp, S. J., & VandeCreek, L. D. (2006). *Practical ethics for psychologists: A positive approach.* Washington, DC: American Psychological Association.

Kvaal, S., Choca, J., & Groth-Marnat, G. (2003). The integrated psychological report. In L. E. Beutler & G. Groth-Marnat (Eds.), *Integrative assessment of adult personality* (2nd ed., pp. 398–433). New York: Guilford Press.

Lacks, P. (1999). *Bender-Gestalt screening for brain dysfunction* (2nd ed.). New York: Wiley.

Lacks, P. (2000). Visuoconstructive abilities. In G. Groth-Marnat (Ed.), *Neuropsychological assessment in clinical practice* (pp. 401–436). New York: Wiley.

Lally, S. J. (2003). What tests are acceptable for use in forensic evaluations? A survey of experts. *Professional Psychology: Research and Practice, 34,* 491–498.

Lichtenberger, E. O., & Kaufman, A. S. (2004). *Essentials of WPPSI-III assessment.* New York: Wiley.

Lilienfeld, S. O., Wood, J. M., & Garb, H. N. (2000). The scientific status of projective techniques. *Psychological Science in the Public Interest, 1,* 27–66.

Lombardo, E. (2003, August). *Quality of life in patients with breast and brain tumors.* Paper presented at the American Psychological Association Convention, Toronto, Ontario, Canada.

Matarazzo, J. D. (1990, September). Psychological assessment versus psychological testing: Validation from Binet to the school, clinic, and courtroom. *American Psychologist, 45*(9), 999–1017.

McCallum, R. S., & Bracken, B. A. (2005). The Universal Nonverbal Intelligence Test: A multidimensional measure of intelligence. In D. P. Flanagan & P. L. Harrison (Eds.), *Contemporary intellectual assessment: Theories, tests, and issues* (2nd ed., pp. 425–440). New York: Guilford Press.

Meagher, S. E., Grossman, S. D., & Millon, T. (2004). Treatment planning and outcome assessment in adults: The Millon Clinical Multiaxial Inventory-III (MCMI-III). In M. W. Maruish (Ed.), *The use of psychological testing for treatment planning and outcomes assessment* (3rd ed., Vol. 3, pp. 479–508). Mahwah, NJ: Erlbaum.

Meyer, G. J. (2004). The reliability and validity of the Rorschach and Thematic Apperception Test (TAT) compared to other psychological and medical procedures: An analysis of systematically gathered evidence. In M. J. Hilsenroth & D. L. Segal (Eds.), *Comprehensive handbook of psychological assessment: Personality assessment* (Vol. 2, pp. 315–342). Hoboken, NJ: Wiley.

Meyer, G. J., Finn, S. E., Eyde, L. D., Kay, G. G., Kubiszyn, T. W., Moreland, K. L., et al. (1998). *Benefits and costs of psychological assessment in healthcare delivery: Report of the board of professional affairs Psychological Assessment Work Group, Part 1.* Washington, DC: American Psychological Association.

Meyer, G. J., Finn, S. E., Eyde, L. D., Kay, G. G., Moreland, K. L., Dies, R. R., et al. (2001, February). Psychological testing and psychological assessment: A review of evidence and issues. *American Psychologist, 56*(2), 128–165.

Miller, D. J., & Thelen, M. H. (1986). Knowledge and beliefs about confidentiality in psychotherapy. *Professional Psychology: Research and Practice, 17,* 15–19.

Mio, J. S., Barker-Hackett, L., & Tumambing, J. (2006). Multicultural psychology: Understanding our diverse communities. New York: McGraw-Hill.

Moretti, R. J., & Rossini, E. D. (2004). The Thematic Apperception Test (TAT). In M. J. Hilsenroth & D. L. Segal (Eds.), *Comprehensive handbook of psychological assessment: Personality assessment* (Vol. 2, pp. 356–371). Hoboken, NJ: Wiley.

Morey, L. C. (2003). *Essentials of PAI assessment.* Hoboken, NJ: Wiley.

Ollendick, T. H., Alvarez, H. K., & Greene, R. W. (2004). Behavioral assessment: History of underlying concepts and methods. In S. N. Haynes & E. M. Heiby (Eds.), *Comprehensive handbook of psychological assessment: Behavioral assessment* (Vol. 3, pp. 19–34). Hoboken, NJ: Wiley.

O'Neill, P. (1998). *Negotiating consent in psychotherapy.* New York: New York University Press.

Pelham, W. E., Fabiano, G. A., & Massetti, G. M. (2005). Evidence-based assessment of attention deficit hyperactivity disorder in children and adolescents. *Journal of Clinical Child and Adolescent Psychology, 34,* 449–476.

Pierro, A., Mannetti, L., Kruglanski, A. W., & Sleeth-Keppler, D. (2004, February). Relevance override: On the reduced impact of "Cues" under high-motivation conditions of persuasion studies. *Journal of Personality and Social Psychology, 86*(2), 251–264.

Pomerantz, A. M. (2005). Increasingly informed consent: Discussing distinct aspects of psychotherapy at different points in time. *Ethics & Behavior, 15,* 351–360.

Pomerantz, A. M., & Handelsman, M. M. (2004). Informed consent revisited: An updated written question format. *Professional Psychology: Research and Practice, 35,* 201–205.

Reisman, J. M. (1991). *A history of clinical psychology* (2nd ed). New York: Hemisphere.

Retzlaff, P. D., & Dunn, T. (2003). The Millon Clinical Multiaxial Inventory-III. In L. E. Beutler & G. Groth-Marnat (Eds.), *Integrative assessment of adult personality* (2nd ed., pp. 192–226). New York: Guilford Press.

Rose, T., Kaser-Boyd, N., & Maloney, M. P. (2001). *Essentials of Rorschach assessment.* New York: Wiley.

Schneider, W., Buchheim, P., Cierpka, M., Dahlbender, R. W., Freyberger, H. J., Grande, T., et al. (2002). Operationalized psychodynamic diagnostics: A new diagnostic approach in psychodynamic psychotherapy. In L. E. Beutler & M. L. Malik (Eds.), *Rethinking the DSM: A psychological perspective* (Decade of behavior) (pp. 177–200). Washington, DC: American Psychological Association.

Seligman, M. E. P., & Csikszentmihalyi, M. (2000). Positive psychology: An introduction. *American Psychologist, 55,* 5–14.

Sherry, A., Dahlen, E., & Holaday, M. (2004). The use of sentence completion tests with adults. In M. J. Hilsenroth & D. L. Segal (Eds.), *Comprehensive handbook of psychological assessment: Personality assessment* (Vol. 2, pp. 372–386). Hoboken, NJ: Wiley.

Simons, H. W. (2001). *Persuasion in society.* Thousand Oaks, CA: Sage.

Sommers-Flanagan, R., & Sommers-Flanagan, J. (1999). *Clinical interviewing* (2nd ed.). New York: Wiley.

Sternberg, R. J. (2000). The concept of intelligence. In R. J. Sternberg (Ed.), *Handbook of intelligence* (pp. 3–15). Cambridge: Cambridge University Press.

Storandt, M., & VandenBos, G. R. (Eds.). (1994). *Neuropsychological assessment of dementia and depression in older adults: A clinician's guide.* Washington, DC: American Psychological Association.

Strunk, W., Jr., & White, E. B. (2000). *The elements of style* (4th ed.). New York: Allyn & Bacon.

Sue, D. W., & Sue, D. (2003). *Counseling the culturally diverse* (4th ed.). New York: Wiley.

Turner, S. M., DeMers, S. T., Fox, H. R., & Reed, G. M. (2001). APA's guidelines for test user qualifications: An executive summary. *American Psychologist, 56,* 1099–1113.

Walsh, W. A. (2007, August). *Understanding patterns of service use and resilience among high-risk children.* Paper presented at the American Psychological Association Convention, San Francisco.

Wasserman, J. D., & Tulsky, D. S. (2005). A history of intelligence assessment. In D. P. Flanagan & P. L. Harrison (Eds.), *Contemporary intellectual assessment: Theories, tests, and issues* (2nd ed., pp. 3–22). New York: Guilford Press.

Watkins, C. E., Campbell, V. L., Nieberding, R., & Hallmark, R. (1995). Contemporary practice of psychological assessment by clinical psychologists. *Professional Psychology: Research and Practice, 26,* 54–60.

Weiner, I. B. (2004). Rorschach Inkblot Method. In M. W. Maruish (Ed.), *The use of psychological testing for treatment planning and outcomes assessment* (3rd ed., Vol. 3, pp. 553–587). Mahwah, NJ: Erlbaum.

Wood, J. (1994). *Gendered lives: Communication, gender, and culture.* Belmont, CA: Wadsworth.

Wood, J. (1999). Gender, communication, and culture. In L. A. Somovar & R. E. Porter (Eds.), *Intercultural communication: A reader* (8th ed., pp. 164–174). Belmont, CA: Wadsworth.

Wood, J. M., Nezworski, M. T., Lilienfeld, S. O., & Garb, H. N. (2003). *What's wrong with the Rorschach?* San Francisco: Jossey-Bass.

World Health Organization (WHO). (2001). Mental functions. In *Body functions, international classification of functioning, disability and health (ICF).* Geneva, Switzerland: Author.

Zhu, J., & Weiss, L. (2005). The Wechsler scales. In D. P. Flanagan & P. L. Harrison (Eds.), *Contemporary intellectual assessment: Theories, tests, and issues* (2nd ed., pp. 297–324). New York: Guilford Press.

Zinsser, W. (2001). *On writing well: The classic guide to writing nonfiction* (25th Anniversary ed.). New York: HarperCollins.

Index

About the Authors

Karen Goldfinger, PhD, is a licensed clinical psychologist with an independent practice in psychotherapy and psychological assessment in Old Saybrook, Connecticut. She has been interested in psychological assessment since graduate school and has completed numerous psychological assessments in inpatient, outpatient, forensic, and educational settings. She has also written psychological assessment manuals, supervised clinical psychology doctoral students and interns in psychological assessment, and taught psychological assessment to doctoral students in a professional psychology program. This textbook is a continuation of her efforts to provide students with the tools they need to conduct effective psychological assessments. She received her PhD in clinical psychology from the State University of New York, Albany.

Andrew M. Pomerantz, PhD, is professor and director of the Clinical Adult Psychology Graduate Program in the Department of Psychology at Southern Illinois University Edwardsville. He is also a licensed clinical psychologist who conducts assessments and psychotherapy in private practice. He is the author of *Clinical Psychology: Science, Practice, and Culture,* a textbook published by SAGE in early 2008, and of ancillary materials for numerous other textbooks in clinical psychology. He has also published articles in *Professional Psychology: Research and Practice, Journal of Clinical Psychology, Teaching of Psychology, Ethics & Behavior,* and other professional journals. He is currently on the editorial board of *Journal of Clinical Psychology.* He received his PhD in clinical psychology from Saint Louis University.